Taste of Home
BUDGET-FRIENDLY
COOKBOOK

TASTE OF HOME BOOKS • RDA ENTHUSIAST BRANDS, LLC • MILWAUKEE, WI

© 2023 RDA Enthusiast Brands, LLC.
1610 N. 2nd St., Suite 102,
Milwaukee WI 53212-3906

Visit us at **tasteofhome.com** for other
Taste of Home books and products.

ISBN: 978-1-62145-951-4

Chief Content Officer, Home & Garden:
Jeanne Sidner
Content Director: Mark Hagen
Creative Director: Raeann Thompson
Senior Editor: Christine Rukavena
Senior Art Director: Courtney Lovetere
Senior Designer: Jazmin Delgado
Deputy Editor, Copy Desk: Dulcie Shoener
Copy Editor: Sara Strauss

Cover Photography:
Photographer: Dan Roberts
Set Stylist: Melissa Franco
Food Stylist: Josh Rink

Pictured on front cover:
Easy Fry Bread Tacos, p. 119

Pictured on title page:
Hamburger Stir-Fry, p. 93

Pictured on back cover:
Marinara Sauce, p. 313; Slow-Cooker
Breakfast Burritos, p. 24; Carolina-Style
Vinegar BBQ Chicken, p. 161; Slow-Cooker
Lava Cake, p. 281; Au Gratin Peas &
Potatoes, p. 256

Printed in China

1 3 5 7 9 10 8 6 4 2

CONTENTS

HOW TO SAVE MONEY ON FOOD

Become a smarter shopper when you brush up on these easy ideas for slashing your grocery bills.

START WITH A PLAN

Create a weekly or monthly food budget. Your grocery bill can eat up between 14 and 34% of your household income. Allocating a certain amount of money for food expenses instantly sets you up for success because you're more likely to seek out sales and less likely to make impulse purchases.

Plan to shop no more than once per week. The fewer times you shop, the more you'll save—on time, gas and money. This also gets you into the cost-saving habit of planning meals for a week, versus ordering pizza, hitting a drive-thru or returning to the store for additional grocery items.

Before shopping, take inventory of your fridge, freezer and pantry. Make a shopping list of what you need and take note of what you don't. That way, you won't impulse-buy an item you already have and won't be wondering about what else you might need. Also, clip any applicable coupons.

In fact, make coupons your new best friends! Pick up a copy of the Sunday paper each week and start clipping, or hit the internet and take advantage of online coupons. Don't forget to make the most of your grocer's weekly specials and membership programs (both print and digital).

When it's time to head for the store, have your shopping list and coupons and a full stomach. You've heard it before, but it bears repeating: Don't go grocery shopping on an empty stomach. The temptation to buy things that aren't on your list can be too great for a hungry shopper to avoid.

7 KEY SHOPPING STRATEGIES

Once you're ready to shop, keep these tips in mind.

1. BUY IN BULK. Consider membership with a warehouse or food club. Buying food and supplies in larger quantities can dramatically cut costs in the long run. Stock up on items such as rice, canned goods and other pantry staples, and watch for specials on family favorite meats you can freeze.

2. LOOK FOR SUBSTITUTES. Saving isn't about cutting out what makes you happy but about shopping smarter. Each time you get back from the store, review your receipts to find the most expensive items. Can you substitute another ingredient, or buy a less expensive brand, in the future?

3. VISIT THE INTERNATIONAL AISLE. You often can find better deals on rice, spices, canned goods, tortillas, beans and other staples in the ethnic aisle than in other areas of the supermarket.

4. KNOW A SALE WHEN YOU SEE IT. When a sale sign catches your attention, think twice before tossing the item into your cart. If something's on sale (even for a great price), but your family doesn't need it or wouldn't enjoy it, then it's not really a good sale for you. If you can't eat the food before it goes bad, that's not a sale for you, either. And two items packaged together at a "special price" isn't a sale if you can buy those items separately for less money.

5. THINK ABOUT BUYING GENERIC. Store brands are usually cheaper than name brands—even when you have a coupon for the name brand. Always compare prices and consider buying generic when possible. If you're concerned about the flavor or quality of a generic item, buy just one item and see if you like it before making it a mainstay in your regular rotation.

6. BE A LOYAL SHOPPER. Variety may be the spice of life, but it isn't the best way to save money when you're buying groceries. Frequenting one store will help you learn about its promotions, such as double-coupon days. And be sure to sign up for any loyalty program that the store offers. Soon you'll be racking up rewards, getting the inside scoop on markdowns and maybe even scoring some freebies!

7. BE AWARE OF AN ITEM'S WEIGHT. No place is better to be concerned about weight than at the grocery store. An item's sticker price can only tell you so much. So look a little closer and check out the unit rate to determine how much the item costs per ounce or pound. Compare different brands, and different amounts between brands, to score the best deal. Buying items with a lower unit rate stretches your food dollars.

CHAPTER 1

BREAKFAST

A hearty and comforting breakfast doesn't have to break the bank. Look here for classic sunrise specialties that use affordable, everyday ingredients. You'll find options for lazy weekends and hurried workdays alike.

TEX-MEX GRAIN BOWL

This recipe is special because it is not only healthy but also delicious. Oatmeal is one of those dishes often eaten sweetened. People rarely think about using it in a savory dish—but they really should!
—Athena Russell, Greenville, SC

TAKES: 20 MIN. • **MAKES:** 4 SERVINGS

4   cups water
2   Tbsp. reduced-sodium taco seasoning
2   cups old-fashioned oats or multigrain hot cereal
1   cup black beans, rinsed, drained and warmed
1   cup salsa
½   cup finely shredded cheddar cheese
1   medium ripe avocado, peeled and cubed
    Optional: Pitted ripe olives, sour cream and chopped cilantro

In a large saucepan, bring water and taco seasoning to a boil. Stir in oats; cook 5 minutes over medium heat, stirring occasionally. Remove from heat. Divide oatmeal among 4 bowls. Top with beans, salsa, cheese, avocado and optional toppings as desired. Serve immediately.

1 SERVING: 345 cal., 13g fat (4g sat. fat), 14mg chol., 702mg sod., 46g carb. (5g sugars, 9g fiber), 12g pro.

TIMESAVING TECHNIQUE

To ripen avocados ASAP, place them in a paper bag with an apple or banana. Poke bag a few times with a toothpick or scissors. Let avocados ripen at room temp 1-2 days. The more fruits added (and ethylene gas they give off), the faster the results.

SIMPLY INCREDIBLE GRITS

Since moving to the South, I have come to love grits! I also love my slow cooker,
and I worked to find a way to make perfect grits without stirring on the stovetop.
I knew this recipe was a winner when my mother-in-law overheard someone at a
church potluck say that it just wasn't right that a Midwesterner could make such good grits!
—*Tacy Fleury, Clinton, SC*

PREP: 10 MIN. • **COOK:** 2½ HOURS • **MAKES:** 6 SERVINGS

Combine the first 6 ingredients in a greased 3-qt. slow cooker. Cook, covered,
on low until liquid is absorbed and grits are tender, 2½-3 hours, stirring every
45 minutes. Stir in cheeses until melted. Serve immediately.

¾ CUP: 334 cal., 15g fat (9g sat. fat), 43mg chol., 755mg sod., 38g carb. (3g sugars,
2g fiber), 11g pro.

2⅔ cups water
1½ cups uncooked
     old-fashioned grits
1½ cups 2% milk
 3 Tbsp. butter, cubed
 2 tsp. chicken bouillon granules
½ tsp. salt
 1 cup shredded cheddar cheese
⅓ cup grated Parmesan cheese

EGGS LORRAINE

Super easy and elegant, this is one of
my favorite special-occasion dishes. It's absolutely delicious!
—*Sandra Woolard, DeLand, FL*

PREP: 15 MIN. • **BAKE:** 25 MIN. • **MAKES:** 2 SERVINGS

1. Preheat oven to 350°. Coat 2 shallow oval 1½-cup baking dishes with cooking spray. Line with Canadian bacon; top with cheese. Carefully break 2 eggs into each dish.

2. In a small bowl, whisk sour cream, salt and pepper until smooth; drop by teaspoonfuls onto eggs.

3. Bake, uncovered, until eggs are set, 25-30 minutes. If desired, sprinkle with chives.

1 SERVING: 258 cal., 18g fat (7g sat. fat), 399mg chol., 687mg sod., 2g carb. (1g sugars, 0 fiber), 22g pro.

4   slices Canadian bacon
2   slices Swiss cheese
4   large eggs
2   Tbsp. sour cream
⅛   tsp. salt
¼   tsp. pepper
    Minced chives, optional

BROWN SUGAR OATMEAL PANCAKES

These pancakes are a favorite at my house. If I don't make them every Saturday and Sunday, the family won't believe it's the weekend! My son's friends often spend the night, and I think it's because they like the pancakes so much. The stacks of jacks are extra delicious served with molasses and syrup.
—*Sharon Bickett, Chester, SC*

TAKES: 15 MIN. • **MAKES:** ABOUT 10 PANCAKES

½ cup plus 2 Tbsp. quick-cooking oats
½ cup whole wheat flour
½ cup all-purpose flour
½ tsp. baking soda
½ tsp. salt
⅓ cup packed brown sugar
1 large egg
2 Tbsp. canola oil
1 cup buttermilk

THRIFTY TIP
Instead of buying buttermilk, you can place 1 Tbsp. white vinegar or lemon juice in a liquid measuring cup and add enough milk to measure 1 cup. Stir, then let stand for 5 minutes. Or, use 1 cup plain yogurt.

1. In a small bowl, combine the oats, flours, baking soda, salt and brown sugar. In another small bowl, beat the egg, oil and buttermilk. Stir into dry ingredients just until moistened.

2. Pour batter by ⅓ cupfuls onto a greased large cast-iron skillet or griddle over medium heat. Turn when bubbles form on top; cook until the second side is golden brown.

FREEZE OPTION: Freeze cooled pancakes between layers of waxed paper in a freezer container. To use, place pancakes on an ungreased baking sheet, cover with foil and reheat in a preheated 375° oven for 5-10 minutes. Or, place a stack of 3 pancakes on a microwave-safe plate and microwave on high until heated through, 1¼-1½ minutes.

2 PANCAKES. 263 cal., 8g fat (1g sat. fat), 44mg chol., 433mg sod., 42g carb. (17g sugars, 3g fiber), 7g pro.

JIFFY CINNAMON ROLLS

I got this recipe from my mom. I like to refrigerate the dough
overnight to quickly bake first thing in the morning.
—Heather Maldaner, Rolling Hills, AB

PREP: 30 MIN. • **BAKE:** 20 MIN. • **MAKES:** 6 ROLLS

1¼ cups all-purpose flour
1 Tbsp. sugar
1 tsp. baking powder
½ tsp. salt
2 Tbsp. cold butter
7 to 8 Tbsp. 2% milk

FILLING
2 Tbsp. plus 2 tsp. butter,
softened, divided
⅓ cup packed brown sugar
1 tsp. ground cinnamon

1. In a bowl, combine the flour, sugar, baking powder and salt. Cut in cold butter until crumbly. Stir in milk, a tablespoon at a time, and toss with a fork until mixture forms a ball. Turn dough onto a lightly floured surface; roll into a 7-in. square. Spread with 2 Tbsp. softened butter.

2. Combine the brown sugar and cinnamon; sprinkle over butter. Roll up jelly-roll style. Cut into 6 even slices. Place cut side up in greased muffin cups. Bake at 400° for 18-20 minutes or until golden brown. Melt remaining butter; brush over rolls. Serve warm.

1 SERVING: 239 cal., 10g fat (6g sat. fat), 26mg chol., 367mg sod., 35g carb. (15g sugars, 1g fiber), 3g pro.

MY TWO CENTS
"I added raisins and glazed the rolls with a mixture of orange juice and add confectioners' sugar. They were absolutely delicious and gone in 5 minutes!"

—EVI.CLAGG, TASTEOFHOME.COM

HONEY-OAT GRANOLA BARS

My husband and I enjoy these bars every day. It's a basic recipe to which you can add
any of your favorite flavors. Try them with coconut or different kinds of chips, nuts and dried fruits.
—*Jean Boyce, New Ulm, MN*

PREP: 15 MIN. • **BAKE.** 15 MIN. ɪ COOLING • **MAKES:** 3 DOZEN

1. Preheat oven to 350°. In a large bowl, combine oats, brown sugar, peanuts, chocolate chips and sunflower kernels. Stir in butter, honey and vanilla until combined (mixture will be crumbly). Press into a greased parchment-lined 15x10x1-in. baking pan.

2. Bake until lightly browned, 15-20 minutes. Cool 15 minutes in pan on a wire rack; cut into bars. Cool completely before removing from pan.

FREEZE OPTION: Transfer cooled bars to an airtight container. Cover and freeze for up to 2 months. To use, thaw bars at room temperature.

1 BAR: 167 cal., 9g fat (4g sat. fat), 10mg chol., 54mg sod., 21g carb. (14g sugars, 2g fiber), 3g pro. **DIABETIC EXCHANGES:** 1½ starch, 1½ fat.

- 4   cups quick-cooking oats
- 1   cup packed brown sugar
- 1   cup chopped salted peanuts
- 1   cup semisweet chocolate chips
- ½   cup sunflower kernels
- ¾   cup butter, melted
- ⅔   cup honey
- 1   tsp. vanilla extract

BLUEBERRY CRUNCH BREAKFAST BAKE

Blueberries in season make this a very special breakfast, but I find that frozen berries can work just as well. My grandmother used to make this with strawberries, and I always loved to eat it at her house.
—Marsha Ketaner, Henderson, NV

PREP: 15 MIN. • **BAKE:** 30 MIN. • **MAKES:** 12 SERVINGS

1   loaf (16 oz.) day-old
    French bread, cut into 1-in. slices
8   large eggs
1   cup half-and-half cream
½   tsp. vanilla extract
1   cup old-fashioned oats
1   cup packed brown sugar
¼   cup all-purpose flour
½   cup cold butter
2   cups fresh or frozen blueberries
1   cup chopped walnuts

1. Arrange half the bread slices in a greased 13x9-in. baking dish.

2. In a large bowl, whisk the eggs, cream and vanilla. Slowly pour half the cream mixture over the bread. Top with remaining bread and egg mixture. Let stand until liquid is absorbed, about 5 minutes.

3. Meanwhile, in a small bowl, combine the oats, brown sugar and flour; cut in butter until crumbly. Sprinkle over top. Top with blueberries and walnuts.

4. Bake, uncovered, at 375° until a knife inserted in the center comes out clean, 30-35 minutes. Let stand for 5 minutes before serving.

1 SERVING: 427 cal., 21g fat (8g sat. fat), 154mg chol., 351mg sod., 50g carb. (23g sugars, 3g fiber), 12g pro.

SAVE SOME CASH

Instead of using 1 cup walnuts, sprinkle this recipe with a nutty homemade streusel topping. Mix ¼ cup each of flour, oats, brown sugar and finely chopped nuts of choice (or shredded coconut), then cut in ¼ cup cold butter. This adds a pretty, crunchy topping while stretching a pricey ingredient. Or just leave the walnuts off and let the blueberries shine.

SAUSAGE & PANCAKE BAKE

Trial and error made this recipe one that my family asks for time and time again. It's so easy and very good.
—Ethel Sanders, Oklahoma City, OK

PREP: 15 MIN. • **BAKE:** 30 MIN. • **MAKES:** 8 SERVINGS

1. Preheat oven to 350°. In a large skillet over medium heat, cook and crumble sausage until no longer pink, 5-7 minutes; drain. Mix biscuit mix, milk, eggs and oil until blended; stir in sausage. Transfer biscuit mixture to a greased 13x9-in. baking dish. Top with apples; sprinkle with cinnamon sugar. Bake until set, 30-45 minutes. Serve with syrup.

TO MAKE AHEAD: Refrigerate, covered, several hours or overnight. To use, preheat oven to 350°. Remove casserole from refrigerator; uncover and let stand while oven heats. Bake as directed, increasing time as necessary until a knife inserted in the center comes out clean.

1 PIECE: 379 cal., 24g fat (6g sat. fat), 80mg chol., 692mg sod., 30g carb. (9g sugars, 1g fiber), 11g pro.

- 1   lb. bulk pork sausage
- 2   cups biscuit/baking mix
- 1⅓ cups 2% milk
- 2   large eggs
- ¼   cup canola oil
- 2   medium apples, peeled and thinly sliced
- 2   Tbsp. cinnamon sugar
      Maple syrup

Save money by making your own biscuit/baking mix. Recipe on p. 304.

MY TWO CENTS

"Absolutely fantastic. It fills the kitchen with a wonderful cinnamon-apple aroma. I easily cut the recipe in half since there are only 2 of us in the house. We will be eating this again."

—MOUSE20650, TASTEOFHOME.COM

FIESTA SCRAMBLED EGGS

I love to fix this spicy scrambled egg dish for friends and family. It's almost a meal
in itself, but I serve it with muffins or biscuits, fresh fruit juice and coffee.
—*Kay Kropff, Canyon, TX*

TAKES: 30 MIN. • **MAKES:** 6 SERVINGS

In a large cast-iron or other heavy skillet, heat oil over medium-high heat. Add onion and peppers; cook and stir until tender, 3-5 minutes. Sprinkle with bacon. Pour eggs over the top; sprinkle with ½ cup cheese, salt and pepper. Cook over medium heat, stirring occasionally, until eggs are completely set. Sprinkle with remaining cheese. Serve with salsa.

NOTE: Wear disposable gloves when cutting hot peppers; the oils can burn skin. Avoid touching your face.

¾ CUP: 254 cal., 19g fat (7g sat. fat), 278mg chol., 609mg sod., 3g carb. (1g sugars, 0 fiber), 17g pro.

1 Tbsp. canola oil
⅓ cup chopped onion
¼ cup chopped sweet red pepper
1 jalapeno pepper, seeded
   and chopped
8 bacon strips, cooked
   and crumbled
8 large eggs, lightly beaten
1 cup shredded
   cheddar cheese, divided
½ tsp. salt
⅛ tsp. pepper
   Salsa

CREAMY BANANA CREPES

My husband and I enjoy taking turns fixing weekend breakfasts. These crepes are frequently on our menus. The sweet-and-sour banana filling is delicious. You'll want to serve them for lunch, dinner and dessert!
—*Parrish Smith, Lincoln, NE*

PREP: 15 MIN. + CHILLING • **COOK:** 15 MIN. • **MAKES:** 6 SERVINGS

2 large eggs
¾ cup water
¾ cup 2% milk
2 Tbsp. butter, melted
½ tsp. vanilla extract
1 cup all-purpose flour
1 Tbsp. sugar
½ tsp. salt

BANANA FILLING

3 Tbsp. butter
3 Tbsp. brown sugar
3 medium firm bananas,
cut into ¼-in. slices

SOUR CREAM FILLING

1 cup sour cream
2 Tbsp. confectioners' sugar
½ cup slivered almonds, toasted

1. In a small bowl, whisk eggs, water, milk, butter and vanilla. In another bowl, mix flour, sugar and salt; add to egg mixture and mix well. Refrigerate, covered, 1 hour.

2. Heat a lightly greased 8-in. skillet over medium heat. Stir batter. Fill a ¼-cup measure three-fourths full with batter; pour into center of pan. Quickly lift and tilt pan to coat bottom evenly. Cook until top appears dry; turn crepe over and cook until bottom is cooked, 15-20 seconds longer. Remove to a wire rack. Repeat with remaining batter, greasing pan as needed. When crepes are cool, stack them between pieces of waxed paper or paper towels.

3. In a small skillet, heat butter and brown sugar over medium heat until sugar is dissolved. Add bananas; toss to coat. Remove from heat; keep warm.

4. In a small bowl, combine sour cream and confectioners' sugar. Spread over half of each crepe. Top with banana filling and almonds; fold crepe over filling. If desired, sprinkle with additional confectioners' sugar and almonds.

2 CREPES: 429 cal., 25g fat (12g sat. fat), 99mg chol., 327mg sod., 46g carb. (22g sugars, 3g fiber), 9g pro.

OVERNIGHT SAUSAGE & GRITS

This recipe is so appealing because you can make it the night before and then pop it into the oven an hour before you want to eat. It works well as a side with pancakes or waffles, but you can also make it the main course for brunch events.
—*Susan Ham, Cleveland, TN*

PREP: 10 MIN. + CHILLING • **BAKE:** 1 HOUR • **MAKES:** 12 SERVINGS

1. Mix grits, cheese and sausage. Beat eggs and milk; stir into grits. Add butter and garlic powder. Transfer to a greased 13x9-in. baking dish. Refrigerate, covered, 8 hours or overnight.

2. Remove dish from refrigerator 30 minutes before baking. Preheat oven to 350°. Bake, uncovered, until a knife inserted in center comes out clean, about 1 hour. Let stand 5 minutes before cutting.

1 PIECE: 259 cal., 19g fat (10g sat. fat), 104mg chol., 491mg sod., 11g carb. (2g sugars, 0 fiber), 11g pro.

3 cups hot cooked grits
2½ cups shredded cheddar cheese
1 lb. bulk pork sausage,
  cooked and crumbled
3 large eggs
1½ cups 2% milk
3 Tbsp. butter, melted
¼ tsp. garlic powder

PUMPKIN SPICE OATMEAL

There's nothing like a warm cup of oatmeal in the morning, and my spiced version works in a slow cooker. Store leftovers in the fridge.
—*Jordan Mason, Brookville, PA*

PREP: 10 MIN. • **COOK:** 5 HOURS • **MAKES:** 6 SERVINGS

In a large bowl, combine the first 6 ingredients; stir in water and milk. Transfer to a greased 3-qt. slow cooker. Cook, covered, on low 5-6 hours or until oats are tender, stirring once. Serve with toppings as desired.

1 CUP: 183 cal., 3g fat (1g sat. fat), 5mg chol., 329mg sod., 34g carb. (13g sugars, 5g fiber), 6g pro. **DIABETIC EXCHANGES:** 2 starch, ½ fat.

1   can (15 oz.) pumpkin
1   cup steel-cut oats
3   Tbsp. brown sugar
1½ tsp. pumpkin pie spice
1   tsp. ground cinnamon
¾ tsp. salt
3   cups water
1½ cups 2% milk
   Optional toppings: Toasted chopped pecans, ground cinnamon, and additional brown sugar and milk

DIY SPICE BLEND
You can make your own pumpkin pie spice with a blend of 4 tsp. cinnamon, 2 tsp. ginger, and 1 tsp. each of ground nutmeg and cloves or allspice. Store in an airtight container in a cool, dry place for up to 6 months.

SLOW-COOKER BREAKFAST BURRITOS

Prep these tasty, hearty burritos the night before for a quick breakfast in the morning,
or let them cook while you are away on a weekend afternoon for an easy supper.
—*Anna Miller, Churdan, IA*

PREP: 25 MIN. • **COOK:** 3¾ HOURS + STANDING • **MAKES:** 12 SERVINGS

1 lb. bulk pork sausage
1 pkg. (28 oz.) frozen
  O'Brien potatoes, thawed
2 cups shredded sharp
  cheddar cheese
12 large eggs
½ cup 2% milk
¼ tsp. seasoned salt
⅛ tsp. pepper
12 flour tortillas (8 in.)
  Optional toppings: Salsa,
  sliced jalapenos, chopped
  tomatoes, sliced green onions
  and cubed avocado

1. In a large skillet, cook sausage over medium heat until no longer pink, 8-10 minutes, breaking into crumbles; drain.

2. In a greased 4- or 5-qt. slow cooker, layer potatoes, sausage and cheese. In a large bowl, whisk eggs, milk, seasoned salt and pepper until blended; pour over top.

3. Cook, covered, on low 3¾-4¼ hours or until eggs are set and a thermometer reads 160°. Uncover and let stand 10 minutes. Serve in tortillas with toppings of your choice.

1 BURRITO: 359 cal., 15g fat (6g sat. fat), 205mg chol., 480mg sod., 39g carb. (2g sugars, 3g fiber), 16g pro.

FRUITY BAKED OATMEAL

This is my husband's favorite breakfast treat and the ultimate comfort food.
It's warm, filling and always a hit when I serve it to guests.
—*Karen Schroeder, Kankakee, IL*

PREP: 15 MIN. • **BAKE:** 35 MIN. • **MAKES:** 9 SERVINGS

1. Preheat oven to 350°. In a large bowl, combine oats, brown sugar, baking powder, salt and cinnamon. Combine eggs, milk and butter; add to the dry ingredients. Stir in apple, peaches and blueberries.

2. Pour into an 8-in. square baking dish coated with cooking spray. Bake, uncovered, until a knife inserted in center comes out clean, 35-40 minutes. Cut into squares. Serve with milk if desired.

NOTE: If using frozen blueberries, use them without thawing to avoid discoloring the mixture.

1 PIECE: 322 cal., 13g fat (7g sat. fat), 75mg chol., 492mg sod., 46g carb. (27g sugars, 3g fiber), 7g pro.

3 cups quick-cooking oats
1 cup packed brown sugar
2 tsp. baking powder
1 tsp. salt
½ tsp. ground cinnamon
2 large eggs, lightly beaten
1 cup fat-free milk
½ cup butter, melted
¾ cup chopped peeled tart apple
⅓ cup chopped fresh or
  frozen peaches
⅓ cup fresh or frozen blueberries
  Additional fat-free milk, optional

MY TWO CENTS
"Delightful. I heat up leftovers for any meal and pour a bit of milk onto it. You can use any fruit you have on hand."

—LJSMILES, TASTEOFHOME.COM

5i
EGG-TOPPED BISCUIT WAFFLES

Breakfast for dinner is always a hit at our house. As a mom, I like transforming
an ordinary breakfast sandwich into something magical and kid-friendly.
—*Amy Lents, Grand Forks, ND*

TAKES: 25 MIN. • **MAKES:** 4 WAFFLES

1½ cups biscuit/baking mix
¾ cup shredded Swiss cheese
⅛ tsp. pepper
½ cup 2% milk
4 large eggs
4 bacon strips, cooked
   and crumbled
   Optional: Cubed avocado and
   pico de gallo

*Save money by making your own
biscuit/baking mix. Recipe on p. 304.*

1. Preheat a 4-square waffle maker. Place baking mix, cheese and pepper in
a bowl. Add milk; stir just until moistened. Transfer to a lightly floured surface;
knead gently 4-6 times. Pat or roll the dough into an 8-in. square; cut into four
4-in. squares.

2. Generously grease top and bottom grids of waffle maker. Place 1 portion of
dough on each section of waffle maker, pressing an indentation in each for eggs.

3. Break an egg over each biscuit; sprinkle with bacon. Close lid carefully over
eggs; bake according to manufacturer's directions until biscuits are golden
brown. If desired, top with avocado and pico de gallo.

NOTE: Recipe may also be baked in a round waffle maker. Divide biscuit dough into
4 portions; pat each into a 4½-in. circle. Assemble and cook 1 serving at a time.

1 SERVING: 386 cal., 20g fat (8g sat. fat), 215mg chol., 802mg sod., 33g carb.
(3g sugars, 1g fiber), 19g pro.

VEGETABLE SCRAMBLED EGGS

I like to have friends and family over for a special Sunday brunch, especially when there's a big game on television. These colorful eggs go perfectly with sausage, toasted English muffins and fresh fruit.
— *Marilyn Ipson, Rogers, AR*

TAKES: 10 MIN. • **MAKES:** 2 SERVINGS

4   large eggs, lightly beaten
¼   cup fat-free milk
½   cup chopped green pepper
¼   cup sliced green onions
¼   tsp. salt
⅛   tsp. pepper
1   small tomato, chopped
      and seeded

In a small bowl, combine the eggs and milk. Add green pepper, onions, salt and pepper. Pour into a lightly greased skillet. Cook and stir over medium heat until eggs are nearly set, 2-3 minutes. Add tomato; cook and stir until eggs are completely set.

¾ CUP: 173 cal., 10g fat (3g sat. fat), 373mg chol., 455mg sod., 7g carb. (4g sugars, 2g fiber), 15g pro. **DIABETIC EXCHANGES:** 2 medium-fat meat, 1 vegetable.

CHAPTER 2

APPS, SNACKS & DRINKS

Keeping healthy, satisfying bites on hand that the whole family will love doesn't have to mean a big bill at the checkout. These savory noshes, fun snacks and treats for sharing let you pull out all the stops without breaking the budget.

(5i)
SOUTHERN DEVILED EGGS

Nothing is more simple, or delicious, than these deviled eggs.
I make them for every BBQ, tailgate or picnic, and they're always a hit.
—Ellen Riley, Murfreesboro, TN

TAKES: 20 MIN. • **MAKES:** 1 DOZEN

6   hard-boiled large eggs
2   Tbsp. mayonnaise
2   Tbsp. sweet pickle relish, drained
½   tsp. prepared mustard
¼   tsp. salt
⅛   tsp. pepper
    Optional: Paprika and fresh dill

1. Slice eggs in half lengthwise. Remove yolks; set whites aside. In a small bowl, mash yolks. Stir in the mayonnaise, relish, mustard, salt and pepper.

2. Pipe or spoon mixture into egg whites. Refrigerate until serving. If desired, sprinkle with paprika and dill before serving.

1 STUFFED EGG HALF: 57 cal., 4g fat (1g sat. fat), 94mg chol., 114mg sod., 1g carb. (1g sugars, 0 fiber), 3g pro.

TIMESAVING TIP
You can make deviled eggs up to 2 days in advance. To optimize their freshness, wait to add the yolk filling to the egg whites until you're ready to serve. Simply store the egg whites in an airtight container, and keep the egg yolk filling in a separate airtight container, making sure to press out all the air. When it's time to serve, simply pipe or spoon the mixture into the egg whites!

MINI HAMBURGERS

These hearty snacks are perfect for Sunday afternoon football games and teen parties.
The mini buns are actually store-purchased pan dinner rolls available everywhere.
—Judy Lewis, Sterling Heights, MI

PREP: 15 MIN. • **BAKE:** 25 MIN. • **MAKES:** 40 SERVINGS

½ cup chopped onion
1 Tbsp. butter
1 large egg, lightly beaten
¼ tsp. seasoned salt
¼ tsp. ground sage
¼ tsp. salt
⅛ tsp. pepper
1 lb. lean ground beef
  (90% lean) or ground beef
40 mini buns, split
8 oz. American cheese slices,
  cut into 1½-in. squares,
  optional
40 dill pickle slices, optional

1. In a large skillet, saute onion in butter. Transfer to large bowl; add egg and seasonings. Crumble beef over mixture and mix well. Spread over bottom halves of the buns; replace tops. Place on baking sheets; cover with foil.

2. Bake at 350° for 20 minutes or until meat is no longer pink. If desired, place a cheese square and pickle slice on each hamburger; replace tops and foil. Return hamburgers to the oven for 5 minutes.

1 BURGER: 106 cal., 3g fat (1g sat. fat), 13mg chol., 180mg sod., 14g carb. (0 sugars, 1g fiber), 5g pro.

MY TWO CENTS
"I love the small size, and the flavor of these little treasures is amazing! Plus, they're super quick to throw together and then bake."
—RANFOREVER, TASTEOFHOME.COM

5i
EASY PICKLE DIP

My love for pickles led me to create this dip. It's so easy to whip together. But be warned: It's addicting!
—April Anderson, Forest Lake, MN

TAKES: 10 MIN. • **MAKES:** 3 CUPS

In a small bowl, beat the cream cheese, sour cream and pickle juice until smooth. Stir in pickles and pepper blend. Serve immediately or refrigerate for up to 4 hours. If desired, serve with chips or pretzels.

¼ CUP: 108 cal., 11g fat (6g sat. fat), 24mg chol., 210mg sod., 2g carb. (2g sugars, 0 fiber), 2g pro.

1   pkg. (8 oz.) cream cheese, softened
1   cup sour cream
¼   cup dill pickle juice
1   cup chopped dill pickles
1   tsp. garlic pepper blend
    Optional: Ridged potato chips or pretzels

ITALIAN APPETIZER MEATBALLS

Store-bought spaghetti sauce speeds up the preparation of tender homemade meatballs. Leftovers make terrific sub sandwiches.
—*Rene McCrory, Indianapolis, IN*

PREP: 40 MIN. • **COOK:** 2 HOURS • **MAKES:** 4 DOZEN

2 large eggs, lightly beaten
½ cup dry bread crumbs
¼ cup 2% milk
2 tsp. grated Parmesan cheese
1 tsp. salt
¼ tsp. pepper
⅛ tsp. garlic powder
1 lb. ground beef
1 lb. bulk Italian sausage
2 jars (24 oz. each) spaghetti sauce
Minced fresh parsley, optional

Save money by making your own marinara sauce. Recipe on p. 313.

1. Preheat oven to 400°. In a large bowl, combine first 7 ingredients. Crumble beef and sausage over mixture and mix lightly but thoroughly. Shape into 1-in. balls.

2. Place meatballs on a greased rack in a shallow baking pan. Bake until no longer pink, 15-20 minutes.

3. Transfer meatballs to a 4-qt. slow cooker; add spaghetti sauce. Cover and cook on high for 2-3 hours or until heated through. Garnish with parsley if desired.

1 MEATBALL: 67 cal., 4g fat (1g sat. fat), 20mg chol., 264mg sod., 4g carb. (2g sugars, 1g fiber), 4g pro.

QUICK TORTILLA PINWHEELS

Prepare these easy, cheesy pinwheels several days in advance if desired.
Serve them with your choice of mild or hot salsa or picante sauce.
—*Barbara Keith, Faucett, MO*

PREP: 15 MIN. + CHILLING • **MAKES:** ABOUT 5 DOZEN

Combine the first 6 ingredients in a bowl; spread mixture on 1 side of each tortilla and roll up tightly. Cover and refrigerate for at least 1 hour. Slice into 1-in. pieces. Serve with salsa or picante sauce.

NOTE: Wear disposable gloves when cutting hot peppers; the oils can burn skin. Avoid touching your face.

1 PINWHEEL: 47 cal., 3g fat (2g sat. fat), 6mg chol., 51mg sod., 4g carb. (0 sugars, 0 fiber), 1g pro.

1 cup sour cream
1 pkg. (8 oz.) cream cheese, softened
¾ cup sliced green onions
½ cup finely shredded cheddar cheese
1 Tbsp. lime juice
1 Tbsp. minced seeded jalapeno pepper
8 to 10 flour tortillas (8 in.), room temperature
    Salsa or picante sauce

5i
STRAWBERRY SPRITZER

Three simple ingredients are all you need to create this fresh and fruity summer beverage. It's bound to become a warm-weather favorite.
—*Krista Collins, Concord, NC*

TAKES: 10 MIN. • **MAKES:** 2½ QT.

1 pkg. (10 oz.) frozen sweetened sliced strawberries, thawed
2 liters lemon-lime soda, chilled
1 can (12 oz.) frozen pink lemonade concentrate, thawed

Place the strawberries in a blender; cover and process until pureed. Pour into a large pitcher; stir in the soda and lemonade concentrate. Serve immediately.

1¼ CUPS: 215 cal., 0 fat (0 sal. fat), 0 chol., 31mg sod., 56g carb. (53g sugars, 1g fiber), 0 pro.

MAKE IT YOUR OWN
If you have fresh mint or basil from the garden, add a few sprigs to the pitcher for a fresh herbal taste. Lighten up the spritzer by using seltzer water instead of soda. It's refreshing!

SALMON CREAM CHEESE SPREAD

Here's a delightful hors d'oeuvre that's excellent for any occasion.
The combination of salmon, cream cheese and spices gives it terrific flavor.
—*Raymonde Hebert Bernier, Saint-Hyacinthe, QC*

PREP: 10 MIN. + CHILLING • **MAKES:** 1½ CUPS

6 oz. cream cheese, softened
3 Tbsp. mayonnaise
1 Tbsp. lemon juice
½ tsp. salt
½ tsp. curry powder
¼ tsp. dried basil
⅛ tsp. pepper
1 can (7½ oz.) salmon, drained, bones and skin removed
2 green onions, thinly sliced
   Crackers and chopped vegetables

In a bowl, combine the cream cheese, mayonnaise and lemon juice. Add the salt, curry powder, basil and pepper; mix well. Gently stir in salmon and onions. Cover and refrigerate for at least 1 hour. Serve with crackers and vegetables.

2 TBSP.: 78 cal., 7g fat (2g sat. fat), 17mg chol., 234mg sod., 1g carb. (0 sugars, 0 fiber), 4g pro.

MY TWO CENTS
"I made this with leftover baked salmon. It is so good!"
—TERRY494, TASTEOFHOME.COM

5i 🍎

RAISIN & HUMMUS PITA WEDGES

The best part about this easy hummus appetizer is you can make your own hummus or, if you don't have time, you can purchase some at the store. It's a year-round food that everyone enjoys.
—*Helene Stewart-Rainville, Sackets Harbor, NY*

TAKES: 15 MIN. • **MAKES:** 8 SERVINGS

¼ cup golden raisins
1 Tbsp. chopped dates
½ cup boiling water
2 whole wheat pita breads (6 in.)
⅔ cup hummus
  Snipped fresh dill or dill weed, optional

Save money by making your own hummus. Recipe on p. 311.

1. Place raisins and dates in a small bowl. Cover with boiling water; let stand for 5 minutes. Drain well.

2. Cut each pita into 4 wedges. Spread with hummus; top with raisins, dates and, if desired, dill.

1 WEDGE: 91 cal., 2g fat (0 sat. fat), 0 chol., 156mg sod., 16g carb. (4g sugars, 3g fiber), 3g pro. **DIABETIC EXCHANGES:** 1 starch.

MIX IT UP

Use whatever dried fruits you have on hand for this healthy snack. Regular raisins, chopped apricots and figs are all good options.

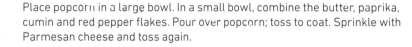

SPICY POPCORN

When I allow myself to indulge in a snack, I make this spicy popcorn. One batch doesn't last long at our house. You can adjust the amount of red pepper flakes to suit your family's tastes.
—*Kay Young, Flushing, MI*

TAKES: 5 MIN. • **MAKES:** 10 SERVINGS

Place popcorn in a large bowl. In a small bowl, combine the butter, paprika, cumin and red pepper flakes. Pour over popcorn; toss to coat. Sprinkle with Parmesan cheese and toss again.

1 CUP: 204 cal., 16g fat (7g sat. fat), 27mg chol., 337mg sod., 13g carb. (0 sugars, 2g fiber), 3g pro.

10 cups popped popcorn
¼   cup butter, melted
 1   tsp. paprika
½   tsp. ground cumin
¼   to ½ tsp. crushed
      red pepper flakes
⅓   cup grated Parmesan cheese

SAVE SOME CASH

Instead of using 2 cans of chickpeas, you can soak and cook 1¾ cups of dried chickpeas according to package directions until tender. Thoroughly pat dry. As a healthy bonus, you can control the snack's sodium content by forgoing canned.

CHILI-LIME ROASTED CHICKPEAS

Looking for a lighter snack that's still a crowd pleaser? You've found it!
These zesty, crunchy chickpeas will have everyone happily munching.
—*Julie Ruble, Charlotte, NC*

PREP: 10 MIN. • **BAKE:** 40 MIN. + COOLING • **MAKES:** 2 CUPS

2 cans (15 oz. each) chickpeas
  or garbanzo beans, rinsed,
  drained and patted dry
2 Tbsp. extra virgin olive oil
1 Tbsp. chili powder
2 tsp. ground cumin
1 tsp. grated lime zest
1 Tbsp. lime juice
¾ tsp. sea salt

1. Preheat oven to 400°. Line a 15x10x1-in. baking sheet with foil. Spread chickpeas in a single layer over foil, removing any loose skins. Bake until very crunchy, 40-45 minutes, stirring every 15 minutes.

2. Meanwhile, whisk together remaining ingredients. Remove chickpeas from oven; let cool 5 minutes. Drizzle with the oil mixture; shake pan to coat. Cool completely. Store in an airtight container.

⅓ CUP: 178 cal., 8g fat (1g sat. fat), 0 chol., 463mg sod., 23g carb. (3g sugars, 6g fiber), 6g pro. **DIABETIC EXCHANGES:** 1½ starch, 1½ fat.

ROSEMARY-SEA SALT CHICKPEAS: Prepare chickpeas according to step 1 in the recipe above. Toss with 2 Tbsp. extra virgin olive oil, 1 Tbsp. minced fresh rosemary and ½ tsp. sea salt.

ORANGE CURRY CHICKPEAS: Prepare chickpeas according to step 1 in the recipe above. Whisk 2 Tbsp. extra virgin olive oil, 1 tsp. grated orange zest and 1 Tbsp. curry powder. Toss chickpeas with oil mixture. Cool completely.

LEMON-PEPPER CHICKPEAS: Prepare chickpeas according to step 1 in the recipe above. Whisk 2 Tbsp. extra virgin olive oil, 1 tsp. grated lemon zest and 2 tsp. freshly ground pepper. Toss chickpeas with oil mixture. Cool completely.

CITRUS & CUCUMBER INFUSED WATER

If you've ever enjoyed cucumber and citrus in a drink before, you know how beautifully they go together. Skip the soda and try this instead for the ultimate in infused water refreshment.
—Taste of Home *Test Kitchen*

PREP: 5 MIN. + CHILLING • **MAKES:** 2 QT.

Combine all ingredients in a large glass carafe or pitcher. Cover and refrigerate 12-24 hours.

½ cup sliced cucumber
½ medium lemon, sliced
½ lime, sliced
½ medium orange, sliced
2 qt. water

PESTO-PEPPER CHEESE SPREAD

I get tons of recipe requests whenever I bring this zippy spread to a party.
Use convenient store-bought pesto or your favorite homemade version.
—*Lara Pennell, Mauldin, SC*

PREP: 25 MIN. + CHILLING • **MAKES:** 3 CUPS

2 pkg. (8 oz. each)
  cream cheese, softened
8 oz. goat cheese, crumbled
2 Tbsp. olive oil
1 tsp. dried thyme
2 garlic cloves, minced
3 Tbsp. prepared pesto
⅓ cup chopped roasted
  sweet red pepper
  Assorted crackers or
  sliced French bread baguette

**Save money by making your
own pesto. Recipe on p. 309.*

1. In a large bowl, combine the cream cheese, goat cheese, oil, thyme and garlic.

2. Line a 1-qt. bowl with plastic wrap. Place a third of the cheese mixture in bowl; top with pesto, half the remaining cheese mixture, the pepper and the remaining cheese mixture. Cover and refrigerate for at least 3 hours.

3. Invert cheese mixture onto a serving plate; discard plastic wrap. Serve with crackers or bread.

¼ CUP: 243 cal., 23g fat (13g sat. fat), 58mg chol., 264mg sod., 2g carb. (1g sugars, 0 fiber), 8g pro.

CHAI TEA

Perfect for cold nights, this masala chai tea recipe incorporates spices that
make it so delicious, you'll want to drink it every day.
—*Kelly Pacowta, Danbury, CT*

TAKES: 20 MIN. • **MAKES:** 4 SERVINGS

4   whole cloves
2   whole peppercorns
4   tea bags
4   tsp. sugar
¼   tsp. ground ginger
1   cinnamon stick (3 in.)
2½ cups boiling water
2   cups 2% milk

1. Place cloves and peppercorns in a large bowl; with the end of a wooden spoon handle, crush spices until aromas are released.

2. Add the tea bags, sugar, ginger, cinnamon stick and boiling water. Cover and steep for 6 minutes. Meanwhile, in a small saucepan, heat the milk.

3. Strain tea, discarding spices and tea bags. Stir in hot milk. Pour into mugs.

1 CUP: 92 cal., 4g fat (2g sat. fat), 12mg chol., 49mg sod., 10g carb. (10g sugars, 0 fiber), 4g pro.

GET YOUR HOT CHAI FIX ON THE GO

It's easy to keep this tea on hand for a quick microwaving whenever you need a cozy hot drink fast. Here's how: Strain the tea, but do not add milk. Cool, then cover and refrigerate for up to 7 days. When ready to serve, pour a 50-50 mix of tea and milk into a microwave-safe mug and cook until hot, about 1½ minutes. Presto! You have a quick coffeehouse treat on the cheap.

WATERMELON SLUSH

This frosty treat makes a refreshing ending to a summer meal.
Simply scoop the slushy mixture into bowls or tall glasses and tip with lemon-lime soda.
—*Elizabeth Montgomery, Allston, MA*

PREP: 5 MIN. + FREEZING • **MAKES:** 8 SERVINGS

¼ cup lime juice
8 cups cubed seedless watermelon
¼ cup sugar
2 cups diet lemon-lime soda, chilled

1. In a blender, cover and process the lime juice, watermelon and sugar in batches until smooth. Pour into a freezer-proof container. Cover and freeze for 30 minutes or until edges begin to freeze.

2. Stir and return to freezer. Repeat every 20 minutes or until slushy, about 90 minutes. Spoon ¾ cup into each bowl or glass; add ¼ cup soda.

1 CUP: 75 cal., 1g fat (0 sat. fat), 0 chol., 12mg sod., 18g carb. (0 sugars, 1g fiber), 1g pro. **DIABETIC EXCHANGES:** 1 fruit.

GET THE MOST JUICE

Next time you squeeze a fresh lemon or lime, warm it in the microwave 7-10 seconds first. Then roll the fruit back and forth under your palm on the counter, giving it firm pressure. You'll get more juice, and the citrus will be easier to squeeze. Works for oranges too.

CHAMPIONSHIP BEAN DIP

My friends and neighbors expect me to bring this irresistible dip to every gathering.
When I arrive, they ask, "You brought your bean dip, didn't you?" If there are any leftovers,
we use them to make bean and cheese burritos the next day.
—*Wendi Wavrin Law, Omaha, NE*

PREP: 10 MIN. • **COOK:** 2 HOURS • **MAKES:** 4½ CUPS

In a large bowl, combine the first 8 ingredients; transfer to a 1½-qt. slow cooker. Cover and cook on high for 2 hours or until heated through, stirring once or twice. Serve with tortilla chips and salsa.

2 TBSP.: 57 cal., 4g fat (2g sat. fat), 12mg chol., 151mg sod., 3g carb. (1g sugars, 1g fiber), 2g pro.

1   can (16 oz.) vegetarian
    refried beans
1   cup picante sauce
1   cup shredded
    Monterey Jack cheese
1   cup shredded cheddar cheese
¾   cup sour cream
3   oz. cream cheese, softened
1   Tbsp. chili powder
¼   tsp. ground cumin
    Tortilla chips and salsa

5i
SAVORY POTATO SKINS

For a simple hot snack on your holiday buffet, put together a plate of these crisp potato skins.
—*Andrea Holcomb, Torrington, CT*

PREP: 1¼ HOURS • **BROIL:** 5 MIN. • **MAKES:** 32 APPETIZERS

4 large baking potatoes
   (about 12 oz. each)
3 Tbsp. butter, melted
1 tsp. salt
1 tsp. garlic powder
1 tsp. paprika
   Optional: Sour cream and chives

1. Preheat oven to 375°. Scrub potatoes; pierce several times with a fork. Place on a greased baking sheet; bake until tender, 1-1¼ hours. Cool slightly.

2. Cut each potato lengthwise in half. Scoop out pulp, leaving ¼-in.-thick shells (save pulp for another use).

3. Cut each half shell lengthwise into quarters; return to baking sheet. Brush insides with butter. Mix seasonings; sprinkle over butter.

4. Broil 4-5 in. from heat until golden brown, 5-8 minutes. If desired, mix sour cream and chives and serve with potato skins.

1 PIECE: 56 cal., 2g fat (1g sat. fat), 6mg chol., 168mg sod., 8g carb. (0 sugars, 1g fiber), 1g pro.

HOT CRAB DIP

I have a large family, work full time, and coach soccer and football, so I appreciate recipes that are easy to assemble. This rich, creamy dip is a fun appetizer to whip up for any gathering.
—Teri Rasey, Cadillac, MI

PREP: 10 MIN. • **COOK:** 3 HOURS • **MAKES:** ABOUT 5 CUPS

In a small bowl, combine milk and salsa. Transfer to a greased 3-qt. slow cooker. Stir in cream cheese, crab, onions and chiles. Cover and cook on low for 3-4 hours, stirring every 30 minutes. Serve with crackers or vegetables.

¼ CUP: 148 cal., 12g fat (7g sat. fat), 38mg chol., 274mg sod., 6g carb. (2g sugars, 0 fiber), 5g pro.

½ cup 2% milk
⅓ cup salsa
3 pkg. (8 oz. each)
   cream cheese, cubed
2 pkg. (8 oz. each)
   imitation crabmeat, flaked
1 cup thinly sliced green onions
1 can (4 oz.) chopped green chiles
   Assorted crackers or
   fresh vegetables

5i
KIDS' FAVORITE PUMPKIN SEEDS

My kids love these pumpkin seeds and want them every fall.
A little bit of pulp in the mix really adds to the flavor, so don't rinse the seeds.
—*Gwyn Reiber, Spokane, WA*

PREP: 5 MIN. • **BAKE:** 45 MIN. + COOLING • **MAKES:** 2 CUPS

1. In a small bowl, combine all ingredients; transfer to an ungreased 15x10x1-in. baking pan.

2. Bake at 250° for 45-50 minutes or until lightly browned and dry, stirring occasionally. Cool completely. Store in an airtight container.

¼ CUP: 122 cal., 9g fat (4g sat. fat), 15mg chol., 158mg sod., 9g carb. (0 sugars, 1g fiber), 3g pro.

2 cups fresh pumpkin seeds
¼ cup butter, melted
½ tsp. garlic salt
¼ tsp. cayenne pepper
¼ tsp. Worcestershire sauce

SCOTCH EGGS

A crispy coating made with cornflakes and pork sausage gives a different
treatment to these hard-boiled eggs. They're fabulous hot out of the oven.
Or enjoy them cold for a snack before a soccer or baseball game.
—*Dorothy Smith, El Dorado, AR*

PREP: 10 MIN. • **BAKE:** 30 MIN. • **MAKES:** 6 SERVINGS

1 lb. bulk pork sausage
    Salt and pepper to taste
6 hard-boiled large eggs
1 large egg, lightly beaten
¾ cup crushed cornflakes

Divide the sausage into 6 portions; flatten and sprinkle with salt and pepper.
Shape each portion around a peeled hard-boiled egg. Roll in beaten egg, then
in cornflake crumbs. Place on a rack in a baking pan. Bake, uncovered, at 400°
for 30 minutes or until meat is no longer pink, turning every 10 minutes.

1 EGG: 283 cal., 20g fat (7g sat. fat), 275mg chol., 463mg sod., 11g carb. (3g sugars,
0 fiber), 14g pro.

SATISFYING SNACK

Wrap leftover Scotch eggs
individually and place them
in an airtight container in the
refrigerator for up to 5 days.
To reheat, cut egg in half and
microwave, cut side down, on
a plate until heated through.

5i
LEMONADE ICED TEA

I have always loved iced tea with lemon, and this delightful thirst quencher just takes it one step further. Lemonade gives the drink a nice color too. I dress up each glass with a slice of lemon on the rim.
—*Gail Buss, New Bern, NC*

PREP: 15 MIN. + CHILLING • **MAKES:** 12 SERVINGS (3 QT.)

In a Dutch oven, bring water to a boil. Remove from the heat; add tea bags. Cover and steep for 5 minutes. Discard tea bags. Stir in sugar and lemonade concentrate. Cover and refrigerate until chilled. Serve over ice. If desired, garnish with lemon slices.

1 CUP: 100 cal., 0 fat (0 sat. fat), 0 chol., 1mg sod., 26g carb. (25g sugars, 0 fiber), 0 pro.

3 qt. water
9 tea bags
¾ to 1¼ cups sugar
1 can (12 oz.) frozen lemonade
   concentrate, thawed
   Lemon slices, optional

TROPICAL PULLED PORK SLIDERS

I used what I had in my cupboard to make this Hawaiian-style pork filling, and the results were fantastic. It's a delicious way to fuel up at a party.
—*Shelly Mitchell, Gresham, OR*

PREP: 15 MIN. • **COOK:** 8 HOURS • **MAKES:** 2 DOZEN

1. Rub roast with garlic and lemon pepper. Transfer to a 4-qt. slow cooker; top with pineapple and orange juice. Cook, covered, on low until meat is tender, 8-10 hours.

2. Remove roast; cool slightly. Skim fat from cooking juices. Shred pork with 2 forks. Return pork and cooking juices to slow cooker. Stir in salsa; heat through. Serve on rolls.

1 SLIDER: 211 cal., 7g fat (2g sat. fat), 34mg chol., 349mg sod., 23g carb. (7g sugars, 3g fiber), 13g pro. **DIABETIC EXCHANGES:** 2 medium-fat meat, 1½ starch.

1 boneless pork shoulder
   butt roast (3 lbs.)
2 garlic cloves, minced
½ tsp. lemon-pepper seasoning
1 can (20 oz.) unsweetened
   crushed pineapple, undrained
½ cup orange juice
1 jar (16 oz.) mango salsa
24 whole wheat dinner rolls, split

5i
PESTO TWISTS

Use pesto made straight from your kitchen garden or purchase it prepared from the grocery store to fill these easy appetizers.
— Jaye Beeler, Grand Rapids, MI

TAKES: 25 MIN. • **MAKES:** 12 TWISTS

1 pkg. (17.3 oz.) frozen puff pastry, thawed
½ cup prepared pesto
½ cup shredded Parmesan cheese Marinara sauce, warmed, optional

Save money by making your own pesto and marinara sauce. Recipes on pp. 309 and 313, respectively.

1. Preheat oven to 400°.

2. Unfold puff pastry sheets on a lightly floured surface. Roll each sheet into a 12-in. square. Spread pesto onto 1 pastry sheet to within ¼ in. of edges. Sprinkle with cheese. Top with remaining pastry, pressing lightly. Cut into twelve 1-in.-wide strips. Twist each strip 4 times. Place 2 in. apart on parchment-lined baking sheets, pressing down ends.

3. Bake until golden brown, 12-15 minutes. Serve warm with marinara sauce, if desired.

1 TWIST: 265 cal., 17g fat (4g sat. fat), 6mg chol., 270mg sod., 24g carb. (0 sugars, 3g fiber), 6g pro.

CHEDDAR TWISTS: Beat 1 large egg and 1 Tbsp. water; brush over both sheets of pastry. Top 1 sheet with ¾ cup shredded cheddar cheese. Top with remaining pastry, egg wash side down. Cut and bake as directed.

SWEET ALMOND TWISTS: Beat 1 large egg and 1 Tbsp. water; brush over both sheets of pastry. Top 1 sheet with ¼ cup almond cake and pastry filling and 1 cup sliced almonds. Top with remaining pastry, egg wash side down. Cut and bake as directed.

GRAPE LEATHER

Instead of giving your kids packaged fruit snacks, offer them homemade fruit leather!
This nutritious treat will stay fresh in a sealed container at room temperature for one month.
—Taste of Home *Test Kitchen*

PREP: 25 MIN. • **BAKE:** 2½ HOURS + COOLING • **MAKES:** 6 SERVINGS

1½ lbs. seedless red grapes
2 Tbsp. sugar
1 Tbsp. lemon juice

1. Sort and wash grapes; remove stems. Place grapes in a steamer basket; place in a large saucepan over 1 in. water. Bring to a boil; cover and steam for 15 minutes or until soft.

2. Preheat oven to 200°. Transfer grapes to a blender or food processor; cover and puree. Strain grapes through a food mill into a small bowl; discard skin. Stir in sugar and lemon juice.

3. Line a 15x10x1-in. baking pan with parchment. Spread fruit mixture evenly onto parchment. Bake 2½-3½ hours or until fruit leather feels slightly sticky. Cool completely.

4. Transfer fruit leather to a new 15x10-in. sheet of parchment. Roll up leather in parchment jelly-roll style, starting with a short side (do not unroll). Cut into six 1½-in. pieces. Store in an airtight container in a cool, dry place up to 1 month.

1 SERVING: 97 cal., 1g fat (0 sat. fat), 0 chol., 2mg sod., 25g carb. (23g sugars, 1g fiber), 1g pro.

5i
CONFETTI SNACK MIX

I've made this party mix for many years, and I usually double the recipe.
It makes a delightful gift, and everyone always asks for the recipe.

—*Jane Dray, Temple Terrace, FL*

TAKES: 10 MIN. • **MAKES:** 7 CUPS

In a large bowl, combine all ingredients. Store in an airtight container.

¼ CUP: 125 cal., 6g fat (3g sat. fat), 1mg chol., 98mg sod., 18g carb. (12g sugars, 1g fiber), 2g pro.

4   cups Golden Grahams
1   cup dry-roasted peanuts
1   cup dried banana chips
1   cup raisins
1   cup milk chocolate M&M's

SWEET & SPICY PEANUTS

With a caramel-like coating and a touch of heat from the hot sauce,
these crunchy peanuts make a tasty anytime snack.
—Taste of Home *Test Kitchen*

PREP: 10 MIN. • **COOK:** 1½ HOURS + COOLING • **MAKES:** 4 CUPS

3 cups salted peanuts
½ cup sugar
⅓ cup packed brown sugar
2 Tbsp. hot water
2 Tbsp. butter, melted
1 Tbsp. Sriracha chili sauce
  or hot pepper sauce
1 tsp. chili powder

1. Place peanuts in a greased 1½-qt. slow cooker. In a small bowl, combine the sugars, water, butter, chili sauce and chili powder. Pour over peanuts. Cover and cook on high for 1½ hours, stirring once.

2. Spread on nonstick aluminum foil to cool. Store in an airtight container.

⅓ CUP: 284 cal., 20g fat (4g sat. fat), 5mg chol., 214mg sod., 22g carb. (16g sugars, 3g fiber), 10g pro.

MY TWO CENTS
"I love this! Maybe next time I will double the hot sauce (just my preference). The treat would be amazing for the holidays or any large gathering."
—APSCHWARTZ, TASTEOFHOME.COM

CHAPTER 3

SOUPS

Hot soup is the ultimate comfort food—a wonderful midday snack or a light meal all by itself. Look here for an assortment of fresh, flavorful, affordable options.

EASY CHILI

This recipe is handy when you want a fast, satisfying meal.
—*Betty-Jean Molyneaux, Geneva, OH*

PREP: 10 MIN. • **COOK:** 40 MIN. • **MAKES:** 6 SERVINGS (2 QT.)

1 lb. ground beef
1 large onion, chopped
2 cans (16 oz. each) kidney beans, rinsed and drained
2 cans (14½ oz. each) diced tomatoes, undrained
1 celery rib, diced
1 tsp. salt
1 tsp. pepper
½ tsp. chili powder
¼ to ½ tsp. crushed red pepper flakes
   Optional: Shredded cheddar cheese, sour cream and chopped green onions

In a large saucepan, cook beef and onion over medium heat until meat is no longer pink, breaking it into crumbles; drain. Stir in the next 7 ingredients. Bring to a boil. Reduce heat; cover and simmer until flavors are blended, about 30 minutes. Top with shredded cheese, sour cream and green onions if desired.

1⅓ CUPS: 308 cal., 9g fat (3g sat. fat), 47mg chol., 908mg sod., 33g carb. (8g sugars, 10g fiber), 24g pro.

CALABRIAN HOLIDAY SOUP

My family is from the Italian region of Calabria; our version of Italian wedding soup has been handed down through the generations. We serve this soup with the Christmas meal as well as at weddings.
—*Gwen Keefer, Sylvania, OH*

PREP: 15 MIN. • **COOK:** 3 HOURS • **MAKES:** 14 SERVINGS (3½ QT.)

1. Place chicken in a 6-qt. stockpot; add water to cover. Slowly bring to a boil. Reduce heat; simmer, covered, 2-3 hours. Meanwhile, in a large bowl, mix 1½ tsp. salt, oregano, basil and 1 tsp. pepper. Add beef; mix lightly but thoroughly. Shape into ½-in. balls.

2. Remove carcass from stockpot; cool. Return broth to a simmer; add meatballs. Cook, uncovered, 8-10 minutes or until meatballs are cooked through.

3. Remove meat from carcass; shred meat with 2 forks and return to pot. Discard carcass and skin. Bring broth to a boil; stir in rice and spinach. Reduce heat; simmer, covered, 5 minutes. Drizzle beaten eggs into soup, stirring constantly. Stir in remaining salt and pepper.

1 CUP: 318 cal., 14g fat (4g sat. fat), 120mg chol., 606mg sod., 18g carb. (0 sugars, 1g fiber), 29g pro.

1   broiler/fryer chicken (4 to 5 lbs.)
3   tsp. salt, divided
1   tsp. dried oregano
1   tsp. dried basil
2½ tsp. pepper, divided
1   lb. lean ground beef (90% lean)
3   cups uncooked instant rice
1   pkg. (10 oz.) frozen chopped spinach, thawed and squeezed dry
3   large eggs, beaten

PUMPKIN & LENTIL SOUP

Plenty of herbs and spices brighten this hearty pumpkin soup.
It's fantastic to enjoy on nippy days and nights.
—*Laura Magee, Houlton, WI*

PREP: 15 MIN. • **COOK:** 7 HOURS • **MAKES:** 6 SERVINGS

1 lb. red potatoes
   (about 4 medium),
   cut into 1-in. pieces
1 can (15 oz.) pumpkin
1 cup dried lentils, rinsed
1 medium onion, chopped
3 garlic cloves, minced
½ tsp. ground ginger
½ tsp. pepper
⅛ tsp. salt
2 cans (14½ oz. each)
   vegetable broth
1½ cups water

In a 3- or 4-qt. slow cooker, combine all ingredients. Cook, covered, on low for 7-9 hours or until potatoes and lentils are tender.

1⅓ CUPS: 210 cal., 1g fat (0 sat. fat), 0 chol., 463mg sod., 42g carb. (5g sugars, 7g fiber), 11g pro. **DIABETIC EXCHANGES:** 3 starch, 1 lean meat.

MY TWO CENTS

"Excellent. I subbed sweet potatoes for the regular potatoes. Warm, hearty and heartwarming! I will be making it again."

—MILLIEANNE, TASTEOFHOME.COM

CREAMY BRATWURST STEW

I adapted a baked stew recipe from the newspaper to create a simple slow-cooked version.
Rich, hearty and creamy, it is the best comfort food for cold winter nights.
Susan Holmes, Germantown, WI

PREP: 20 MIN. • **COOK:** 6½ HOURS • **MAKES:** 8 SERVINGS (2 QT.)

1¾ lbs. potatoes
   (about 4 medium),
   peeled and cubed
2 medium carrots, chopped
2 celery ribs, chopped
1 medium onion, chopped
1 medium green pepper, chopped
2 lbs. uncooked bratwurst links
½ cup chicken broth
1 tsp. salt
1 tsp. dried basil
½ tsp. pepper
2 cups half-and-half cream
1 Tbsp. cornstarch
3 Tbsp. cold water

1. Place first 5 ingredients in a 5-qt. slow cooker; toss to combine. Top with bratwurst. Mix broth and seasonings; pour over top.

2. Cook, covered, on low 6-7 hours until the sausage is cooked through and vegetables are tender. Remove sausages from slow cooker; cut into 1-in. slices. Return sausages to potato mixture; stir in cream.

3. Mix cornstarch and water until smooth; stir into stew. Cook, covered, on high until thickened, about 30 minutes.

1 CUP: 544 cal., 39g fat (15g sat. fat), 114mg chol., 1367mg sod., 25g carb. (5g sugars, 2g fiber), 19g pro.

CREAM OF MUSSEL SOUP

Every New England cook has a personal version of mussel soup, depending on the favored regional herbs and cooking customs. Feel free to start with this recipe and develop your own luscious variation.
—*Donna Noel, Gray, ME*

PREP: 35 MIN. • **COOK:** 10 MIN. • **MAKES:** 5 SERVINGS

3 lbs. fresh mussels
(about 5 dozen), scrubbed
and beards removed
2 medium onions, finely chopped
2 celery ribs, finely chopped
1 cup water
1 cup white wine or chicken broth
1 bottle (8 oz.) clam juice
¼ cup minced fresh parsley
2 garlic cloves, minced
¼ tsp. salt
¼ tsp. pepper
1 cup half-and-half cream

1. Tap mussels; discard any that do not close. Set aside. In a stockpot, combine the onions, celery, water, wine or broth, clam juice, parsley, garlic, salt and pepper.

2. Bring to a boil. Reduce heat; add mussels. Cover and simmer until mussels have opened, 5-6 minutes. Remove mussels with a slotted spoon, discarding any unopened mussels; set aside opened mussels and keep warm.

3. Cool cooking liquid slightly. In a blender, cover and process cooking liquid in batches until blended. Return all to pan. Add cream and reserved mussels; heat through (do not boil).

1 SERVING: 368 cal., 11g fat (4g sat. fat), 102mg chol., 1043mg sod., 20g carb. (6g sugars, 2g fiber), 35g pro.

ITALIAN VEGGIE BEEF SOUP

My sweet father-in-law, Pop Pop, would bring this chunky soup to our house when we were under the weather. We like it so much, we take it to our own friends who need comfort. It always does the trick.
—*Sue Webb, Reisterstown, MD*

TAKES: 30 MIN. • **MAKES:** 12 SERVINGS (4 QT.)

1. In a 6-qt. stockpot, cook ground beef and onions over medium-high heat until beef is no longer pink, 6-8 minutes, breaking beef into crumbles; drain.

2. Add cabbage, mixed vegetables, tomatoes, seasonings and broth; bring to a boil. Reduce heat; simmer, uncovered, until cabbage is crisp-tender, 10-15 minutes. Remove bay leaf.

FREEZE OPTION: Freeze cooled soup in freezer containers. To use, partially thaw in refrigerator overnight. Heat through in a saucepan, stirring occasionally; add a little broth if necessary.

1⅓ CUPS: 159 cal., 5g fat (2g sat. fat), 38mg chol., 646mg sod., 14g carb. (6g sugars, 4g fiber), 15g pro. **DIABETIC EXCHANGES:** 2 lean meat, 1 vegetable, ½ starch.

1½ lbs. lean ground beef (90% lean)
2 medium onions, chopped
4 cups chopped cabbage
1 pkg. (16 oz.) frozen mixed vegetables
1 can (28 oz.) crushed tomatoes
1 bay leaf
3 tsp. Italian seasoning
1 tsp. salt
½ tsp. pepper
2 cartons (32 oz. each) reduced-sodium beef broth

HOMEMADE TURKEY SOUP

You can make the most of even the smallest pieces of leftover holiday turkey with this homemade soup. I simmer the bones to get the rich flavor, then easily remove any meat that remains. I add rice, vegetables and cream soup for a hearty meal that's tasty and economical.
—*June Sangrey, Manheim, PA*

PREP: 30 MIN. • **COOK:** 2½ HOURS • **MAKES:** 10 SERVINGS (ABOUT 2½ QT.)

1 leftover turkey carcass (from a 10- to 12-lb. turkey)
2 qt. water
1 medium onion, cut into wedges
½ tsp. salt
2 bay leaves
1 cup chopped carrots
1 cup uncooked long grain rice
⅓ cup chopped celery
¼ cup chopped onion
1 can (10½ oz.) condensed cream of chicken or cream of mushroom soup, undiluted

1. Place the turkey carcass in a stockpot; add the water, onion wedges, salt and bay leaves. Slowly bring to a boil over low heat; cover and simmer for 2 hours.

2. Remove carcass; cool. Strain broth and skim fat. Discard onion and bay leaves. Return broth to the pan. Add the carrots, rice, celery and chopped onion; cover and simmer until rice and vegetables are tender.

3. Remove turkey from bones; discard bones and cut turkey into bite-sized pieces. Add turkey and cream soup to broth; heat through.

1 CUP: 128 cal., 2g fat (1g sat. fat), 3mg chol., 391mg sod., 21g carb. (1g sugars, 1g fiber), 3g pro.

MY TWO CENTS
"Easy and delicious! Wonderful way to use a turkey carcass. I added peas and a little more seasoning."
—MGLAHTI, TASTEOFHOME.COM

EASY WHITE CHICKEN CHILI

Chili is one of our best cold-weather strategies. We use chicken and white
beans for a twist on the regular bowl of red. It's soothing comfort food.
—*Rachel Lewis, Danville, VA*

TAKES: 30 MIN. • **MAKES:** 6 SERVINGS

1. In a large saucepan, cook chicken and onion over medium-high heat until chicken is no longer pink, 6-8 minutes, breaking chicken into crumbles.

2. Pour 1 can of beans in a small bowl; mash slightly. Stir the mashed beans, remaining can of beans, chiles, seasonings and broth into chicken mixture; bring to a boil. Reduce heat; simmer, covered, until flavors are blended, 12-15 minutes. Serve with toppings as desired.

FREEZE OPTION: Freeze cooled chili in freezer containers. To use, partially thaw in refrigerator overnight. Heat through in a saucepan, stirring occasionally; add broth if necessary.

1 CUP: 228 cal., 5g fat (1g sat. fat), 54mg chol., 504mg sod., 23g carb. (1g sugars, 6g fiber), 22g pro. **DIABETIC EXCHANGES:** 3 lean meat, 1½ starch.

1   lb. lean ground chicken
1   medium onion, chopped
2   cans (15 oz. each)
    cannellini beans,
    rinsed and drained
1   can (4 oz.) chopped green chiles
1   tsp. ground cumin
½   tsp. dried oregano
¼   tsp. pepper
1   can (14½ oz.) reduced-sodium
    chicken broth
    Optional toppings:
    Reduced-fat sour cream,
    shredded cheddar cheese and
    chopped fresh cilantro

PESTO MINESTRONE

I rely on store-bought pesto to provide mild flavor in this chunky tortellini and vegetable soup.
It's a hit in my house. If you don't like zucchini, use another vegetable.
—*Natalie Cataldo, Des Moines, IA*

TAKES: 30 MIN • **MAKES:** 4 SERVINGS

½ cup chopped onion
2 tsp. olive oil
1 tsp. minced garlic
2¼ cups water
2 cups frozen mixed vegetables
1 can (14½ oz.) vegetable broth
¾ tsp. dried oregano
½ tsp. salt
½ tsp. pepper
1 pkg. (9 oz.) refrigerated cheese tortellini
2 cups diced zucchini
2 Tbsp. prepared pesto

*Save money by making your own pesto. Recipe on p. 309.

1. In a large saucepan, saute onion in oil until tender. Add garlic; cook 1 minute longer. Stir in the water, mixed vegetables, broth, oregano, salt and pepper. Bring to a boil. Reduce heat; cover and simmer for 3 minutes.

2. Add the tortellini, zucchini and pesto. Simmer, uncovered, 7-9 minutes longer or until pasta and vegetables are tender.

1 CUP: 337 cal., 12g fat (4g sat. fat), 30mg chol., 1063mg sod., 47g carb. (8g sugars, 7g fiber), 15g pro.

SLOW-COOKER HOMEMADE CHICKEN & RICE SOUP

Using the slow cooker takes some of the effort out of making from-scratch
chicken soup. The long cook time helps develop superb homemade flavor.
—Kevin Bruckerhoff, Columbia, MO

PREP: 15 MIN. • **COOK:** 7 HOURS • **MAKES:** 16 SERVINGS (4 QT.)

3   qt. water
4   bone-in chicken breast
    halves (about 3 lbs.)
1½ tsp. salt
¼   tsp. pepper
¼   tsp. poultry seasoning
1   tsp. chicken bouillon granules
3   medium carrots, chopped
2   celery ribs, chopped
1   small onion, chopped
½   cup uncooked converted rice
    Minced fresh parsley, optional

1. In a 6-qt. slow cooker, place water, chicken, salt, pepper and poultry seasoning. Cover and cook on low 6-7 hours or until chicken is tender.

2. With a slotted spoon, remove chicken from broth. When cool enough to handle, remove meat from bones; discard skin and bones. Cut chicken into bite-sized pieces. Skim fat from broth; add chicken and next 5 ingredients. Cover and cook on high 1-2 hours or until vegetables and rice are tender. If desired, sprinkle each serving with parsley.

1 CUP: 202 cal., 6g fat (2g sat. fat), 66mg chol., 513mg sod., 10g carb. (1g sugars, 1g fiber), 25g pro.

SALTY SOUP RESCUE

Next time you accidentally oversalt your soup, toss in a few wedges of raw apple or potato. Simmer for 10 minutes, then discard the wedges—along with the excess salt.

CRAB CORN CHOWDER

No time to make a homemade soup? Think again! You'll be ladling out steamy bowls of satisfying chowder in no time. Canned corn and crab blend beautifully in this creamy, colorful soup.
—*Sarah McClanahan, Raleigh, NC*

PREP: 15 MIN. • **COOK:** 20 MIN. • **MAKES:** 8 SERVINGS (2 QT.)

1. Dissolve bouillon in water; set aside. In a Dutch oven, cook bacon over medium heat until crisp. Remove bacon to paper towels to drain, reserving drippings.

2. In the same pan, saute peppers and onion in drippings until tender. Stir in flour. Gradually stir in bouillon mixture. Bring to a boil; cook and stir for 2 minutes or until thickened.

3. Reduce heat; gradually stir in cream and corn. Add the seasoned salt, basil and cayenne. Cook until heated through, stirring occasionally (do not boil). Stir in the crab. Top each serving with bacon and chives.

1 SERVING: 290 cal., 12g fat (7g sat. fat), 88mg chol., 1195mg sod., 28g carb. (8g sugars, 2g fiber), 16g pro.

- 3 tsp. chicken bouillon granules
- 2 cups boiling water
- 6 bacon strips, diced
- ⅓ cup each diced sweet red, yellow and orange peppers
- ½ cup chopped onion
- ¼ cup all-purpose flour
- 3 cups half-and-half cream
- 2 cans (14¾ oz. each) cream-style corn
- 1½ tsp. seasoned salt
- ½ tsp. dried basil
- ¼ to ½ tsp. cayenne pepper
- 2 cans (6 oz. each) crabmeat, drained, flaked and cartilage removed or 2 cups flaked imitation crabmeat
- ½ cup minced chives or green onions

LENTIL SPINACH SOUP

Protein-packed lentils are a delicious alternative to beans in this simple, nutritious soup.
—*Margaret Wilson, San Bernardino, CA*

PREP: 15 MIN. • **COOK:** 30 MIN. • **MAKES:** 5 SERVINGS

½ lb. bulk Italian turkey sausage
1 small onion, chopped
4 cups water
½ cup dried lentils, rinsed
2 tsp. chicken bouillon granules
⅛ tsp. crushed red pepper flakes
1 pkg. (10 oz.) fresh spinach, coarsely chopped
2 Tbsp. shredded Parmesan cheese

In a large saucepan, cook sausage and onion until meat is no longer pink, breaking meat into crumbles; drain. Stir in water, lentils, bouillon and red pepper flakes; bring to a boil. Reduce heat; cover and simmer for 25-30 minutes or until lentils are tender. Stir in spinach; cook 3-5 minutes longer or until spinach is tender. Sprinkle with cheese.

1 CUP: 136 cal., 4g fat (1g sat. fat), 18mg chol., 632mg sod., 15g carb. (1g sugars, 3g fiber), 11g pro. **DIABETIC EXCHANGES:** 1 starch, 1 lean meat.

THRIFTY TIP

Lentils are an economical, healthy way to stretch the meat in a recipe. Here the lentils contribute 4g of protein, plus 2g of healthy fiber, to each cup of soup!

SOUTHWESTERN BEEF BARLEY STEW

Hearty and easy to fix, this thick stew has a comforting, chili-like flavor. It's
my best barley recipe. I'm sure you'll agree that it's a tasty dish.
—Lisa Kolenich, Regina, SK

TAKES: 30 MIN. • **MAKES:** 3 SERVINGS

½ lb. lean ground beef (90% lean)
½ cup sliced celery
⅓ cup chopped onion
1¾ cups water
2 tsp. reduced-sodium
  beef bouillon granules
1½ tsp. chili powder
¼ tsp. pepper
½ cup quick-cooking barley
1 can (14½ oz.) diced
  tomatoes, undrained

1. In a large saucepan, cook beef, celery and onion over medium heat until meat is no longer pink and vegetables are tender, breaking meat into crumbles; drain.

2. Stir in the water, bouillon, chili powder and pepper. Bring to a boil. Stir in barley. Reduce heat; cover and simmer for 10-12 minutes or until barley is tender. Stir in tomatoes; heat through.

1⅓ CUPS: 269 cal., 7g fat (3g sat. fat), 37mg chol., 456mg sod., 33g carb. (6g sugars, 9g fiber), 20g pro. **DIABETIC EXCHANGES:** 2 lean meat, 1½ starch, 1 vegetable.

RED BEAN VEGETABLE SOUP

Cajun seasoning boosts the flavor of my bean soup that's loaded with fresh vegetables. Yum!
—*Ronnie Lappe, Brownwood, TX*

PREP: 15 MIN. • **COOK:** 6 HOURS • **MAKES:** 12 SERVINGS (3 QT.)

In a 5-qt. slow cooker, combine the peppers, celery, onions and beans. Stir in the remaining ingredients. Cover and cook on low for 6 hours or until vegetables are tender. Discard bay leaves before serving.

1 CUP: 158 cal., 0 fat (0 sat. fat), 2mg chol., 701mg sod., 29g carb. (5g sugars, 8g fiber), 11g pro.

3 large sweet red peppers, chopped
3 celery ribs, chopped
2 medium onions, chopped
4 cans (16 oz. each) kidney beans, rinsed and drained
4 cups chicken broth
2 bay leaves
½ to 1 tsp. salt
½ to 1 tsp. Cajun seasoning
½ tsp. pepper
¼ to ½ tsp. hot pepper sauce

BUDGET SPICE BLEND

If you don't have Cajun seasoning on hand, make your own with the spices you have. There are many different blends, but a typical mix will include salt, cayenne pepper, garlic powder, paprika, thyme, pepper and onion powder.

SLOW-COOKER SPLIT PEA SOUP WITH HAM HOCKS

Just let this soup simmer while you are out for the day and a delicious dinner will be ready
when you get home. This is a very hearty soup. The ham hocks lend a smoky flavor.
Taste of Home *Test Kitchen*

PREP: 15 MIN. • **COOK:** 8 HOURS • **MAKES:** 8 SERVINGS (ABOUT 2½ QT.)

---

1   can (49½ oz.) chicken broth
1½ lbs. smoked ham hocks
2   cups each chopped onions,
    celery and carrots
1   pkg. (16 oz.) dried green split peas
2   bay leaves
    Salad croutons, optional

1. In a 4- or 5-qt. slow cooker, combine the broth, ham hocks, vegetables, split peas and bay leaves. Cover and cook on low for 8-10 hours or until ham hocks and peas are tender.

2. Discard bay leaves. Remove meat from bones when cool enough to handle; cut ham into small pieces and set aside. Cool soup slightly.

3. In a blender, cover and process soup in batches until smooth. Return soup to slow cooker; stir in reserved ham. Heat through. Garnish with croutons if desired.

1¼ CUPS: 265 cal., 2g fat (1g sat. fat), 10mg chol., 924mg sod., 44g carb. (9g sugars, 16g fiber), 19g pro.

CHAPTER 4
MAIN COURSES

It's possible to satisfy everyone in the family without busting your budget. These recipes call for popular, economical cuts of meat and poultry, thrifty seafood, and plant-based meatless ingredients. You can't beat each meal's utter deliciousness.

LASAGNA ROLLS

My Italian roll-ups are not complicated; they require just basic ingredients to assemble.
Prepared pasta sauce helps me save time and get dinner on the table sooner.
—*Mary Lee Thomas, Logansport, IN*

PREP: 25 MIN. • **BAKE:** 10 MIN. • **MAKES:** 6 SERVINGS

6 lasagna noodles
1 lb. ground beef
1 jar (14 oz.) pasta sauce
1 tsp. fennel seed, optional
2 cups shredded part-skim
   mozzarella cheese, divided

*Save money by making your own
marinara sauce. Recipe on p. 313.*

1. Cook lasagna noodles according to package directions. Meanwhile, in a large skillet, cook beef over medium heat until no longer pink, breaking it into crumbles; drain. Stir in spaghetti sauce and, if desired, fennel seed; heat through.

2. Drain noodles. Spread ¼ cup meat sauce over each noodle; sprinkle with 2 Tbsp. cheese. Carefully roll up noodles and place seam side down in an 8-in. square baking dish. Top with remaining sauce and cheese.

3. Bake, uncovered, at 400° for 10-15 minutes or until heated through and cheese is melted.

1 SERVING: 377 cal., 18g fat (8g sat. fat), 70mg chol., 549mg sod., 26g carb. (6g sugars, 2g fiber), 28g pro.

MY TWO CENTS
*"I made these with
ricotta added to the
filling—I just dabbed
it on top of the meat
sauce. Yummy!
Another keeper."*
—CATWEBER, TASTEOFHOME.COM

CRUNCHY BURGER QUESADILLAS

We adore burgers—all kinds! We also love quesadillas and tacos. I combined all the above to make scrumptious and very filling burgers that my whole family enjoys.
—*Ann Marie Eberhart, Gig Harbor, WA*

TAKES: 30 MIN. • **MAKES:** 4 SERVINGS

1. Gently shape beef into 4 balls, shaping just enough to keep together (do not compact). In a large skillet, heat oil over medium heat. Working in batches, add beef. With a heavy metal spatula, flatten to ¼- to ½-in. thickness. Cook until edges start to brown, about 1½ minutes. Turn burgers; cook until well browned and a thermometer reads at least 160°, about 1 minute. Repeat with remaining beef. Remove from skillet; wipe skillet clean.

2. Combine mayonnaise and salsa; reserve half for serving. Spread remaining mixture over tortillas. On the center of each tortilla, place 1 slice cheese, 1 burger and 1 tostada shell. Fold sides of tortilla over burger; fold top and bottom to close, pleating as you go.

3. In batches, place wraps in skillet, seam side down. Cook on medium heat 1-2 minutes on each side or until golden brown. Serve with remaining sauce.

1   lb. ground beef
2   tsp. canola oil
1   cup mayonnaise
⅓   cup salsa
4   flour tortillas (12 in.)
4   slices pepper jack or cheddar cheese
4   tostada shells

1 WRAP: 912 cal., 69g fat (17g sat. fat), 93mg chol., 1144mg sod., 41g carb. (2g sugars, 5g fiber), 31g pro.

HAMBURGER STIR-FRY

Here's a quick, easy teriyaki stir-fry that uses hamburger instead of the traditional beef strips.
It has a nice sauce and is different enough to be a treat for the taste buds.
—*Kathie and John Horst, Westfield, NY*

TAKES: 25 MIN. • **MAKES:** 4 SERVINGS

1. In a small bowl, combine sugar, cornstarch and mustard. Stir in water and teriyaki sauce until smooth.

2. In a large nonstick skillet or wok over medium heat, cook beef until no longer pink, 5-7 minutes, breaking into crumbles; drain and set aside. In the same pan, heat oil over medium heat; add vegetable blend and onion. Cook and stir until crisp-tender, 6-8 minutes.

3. Stir cornstarch mixture and add to pan. Bring to a boil; cook and stir until thickened, 1-2 minutes. Add beef; heat through. Serve with rice. Sprinkle with sesame seeds and, if desired, top with green onions.

1 SERVING: 399 cal., 12g fat (4g sat. fat), 56mg chol., 516mg sod., 42g carb. (9g sugars, 3g fiber), 28g pro. **DIABETIC EXCHANGES:** 3 lean meat, 2 starch, 2 vegetable, ½ fat.

1 Tbsp. sugar
1 Tbsp. cornstarch
1 Tbsp. ground mustard
⅓ cup cold water
⅓ cup reduced-sodium teriyaki sauce
1 lb. lean ground beef (90% lean)
2 tsp. canola oil
1 pkg. (16 oz.) frozen asparagus stir-fry vegetable blend
1 medium onion, halved and thinly sliced
2 cups hot cooked rice
2 tsp. sesame seeds
Julienned green onions, optional

GO-TO PANTRY MEALS
Good cooks like to keep the ingredients for a few go-to recipes on hand so a special trip to the store is not required. This good-for-you stir-fry dinner can be one of those recipes. Just keep ground beef and veggies in the freezer and you'll always be ready to whip this up.

HEARTY PENNE BEEF

This is comfort food at its finest! The best of everything is found here—it's
tasty, easy and a smart way to sneak in some spinach for extra nutrition.
—Taste of Home *Test Kitchen*

TAKES: 30 MIN. • **MAKES:** 4 SERVINGS

1¾ cups uncooked penne pasta
1 lb. ground beef
1 tsp. minced garlic
1 can (15 oz.) tomato puree
1 can (14½ oz.) beef broth
1½ tsp. Italian seasoning
1 tsp. Worcestershire sauce
¼ tsp. each salt and pepper
2 cups chopped fresh spinach
2 cups shredded part-skim
   mozzarella cheese

1. Cook pasta according to the package directions. Meanwhile, in a Dutch oven, cook beef over medium heat until no longer pink, breaking it into crumbles. Add garlic; cook 1 minute longer. Drain. Stir in tomato puree, broth, Italian seasoning, Worcestershire sauce, salt and pepper.

2. Bring to a boil. Reduce heat; simmer, uncovered, until slightly thickened, 10-15 minutes. Add spinach; cook until wilted, 1-2 minutes.

3. Drain pasta; stir into beef mixture. Sprinkle with cheese; cover and cook until cheese is melted, 3-4 minutes.

FREEZE OPTION: Freeze cooled pasta mixture in freezer containers. To use, partially thaw in refrigerator overnight. Heat through in a saucepan, stirring occasionally; add broth or water if necessary.

1½ CUPS: 482 cal., 20g fat (10g sat. fat), 88mg chol., 1001mg sod., 33g carb. (5g sugars, 2g fiber), 41g pro.

TIMESAVING TECHNIQUE

A quick way to prep garlic is to smash the cloves with the side of your knife blade, then rock your knife back and forth through the garlic until it's chopped into fine pieces. The technique works fine in rustic dishes like this penne.

EASY SLOW-COOKER POT ROAST

I love pot roast for a couple of reasons. First, it's delicious. Second, it's easy!
I can't describe the feeling of walking into my house after work and smelling this
dish that's been simmering in the slow cooker all day. There's nothing better.
—*James Schend, Pleasant Prairie, WI*

PREP: 10 MIN. • **COOK:** 10 HOURS • **MAKES:** 10 SERVINGS

1. In a large skillet over medium heat, brown roast in oil on all sides. Place carrots, potatoes and onion in a 6-qt. slow cooker. Place the roast on top of vegetables; sprinkle with steak seasoning. Add broth. Cook, covered, on low 10-12 hours, until beef and vegetables are tender.

2. Remove roast and vegetables from slow cooker; keep warm.

3. Transfer cooking juices to a saucepan; skim off fat. Bring juices to a boil. In a small bowl, mix cornstarch and water until smooth; stir into juices. Return to a boil, stirring constantly; cook and stir until thickened, 1-2 minutes. Serve with roast and vegetables.

1 SERVING: 354 cal., 15g fat (5g sat. fat), 88mg chol., 696mg sod., 24g carb. (4g sugars, 3g fiber), 30g pro. **DIABETIC EXCHANGES:** 4 lean meat, 1½ starch, ½ fat.

1 boneless beef rump or
   chuck roast (3 to 3½ lbs.)
1 Tbsp. canola oil
6 medium carrots, cut into thirds
6 medium potatoes, peeled
   and quartered
1 large onion, quartered
3 tsp. Montreal steak seasoning
1 carton (32 oz.) beef broth
3 Tbsp. cornstarch
3 Tbsp. water

ZUCCHINI BEEF SKILLET

This is a speedy summer recipe that uses up those abundant
garden goodies: zucchini, tomatoes and green peppers.
—*Becky Calder, Kingston, MO*

TAKES: 30 MIN. • **MAKES:** 4 SERVINGS

1. In a large skillet, cook beef with onion and pepper over medium-high heat until no longer pink, 5-7 minutes, breaking beef into crumbles; drain.

2. Stir in seasonings, vegetables, water and rice; bring to a boil. Reduce heat; simmer, covered, until the rice is tender, 10-15 minutes. Sprinkle with cheese. Remove from heat; let stand until cheese is melted.

2 CUPS: 470 cal., 24g fat (11g sat. fat), 98mg chol., 749mg sod., 33g carb. (8g sugars, 4g fiber), 32g pro.

1   lb. ground beef
1   medium onion, chopped
1   small green pepper, chopped
2   tsp. chili powder
¾   tsp. salt
¼   tsp. pepper
3   medium zucchini,
    cut into ¾-in. cubes
2   large tomatoes, chopped
¼   cup water
1   cup uncooked instant rice
1   cup shredded cheddar cheese

CORNBREAD TACO BAKE

Cornbread and beef bake together in one casserole dish, making this entree convenient.
It's packed with tempting seasonings, and the cheese and onions make an attractive topping.
—*Vicki Good, Oscoda, MI*

PREP: 20 MIN. • **BAKE:** 25 MIN. • **MAKES:** 6 SERVINGS

1½ lbs. ground beef
1 can (15¼ oz.) whole kernel corn, drained
1 can (8 oz.) tomato sauce
½ cup water
½ cup chopped green pepper
1 envelope taco seasoning
1 pkg. (8½ oz.) cornbread/muffin mix
1 can (2.8 oz.) french-fried onions, divided
⅓ cup shredded cheddar cheese

1. In a large skillet, cook beef over medium heat until no longer pink, breaking it into crumbles; drain. Stir in the corn, tomato sauce, water, green pepper and taco seasoning. Spoon into a greased 2-qt. baking dish.

2. Prepare cornbread mix according to package directions for cornbread. Stir in half the onions. Spread over beef mixture. Bake, uncovered, at 400° for 20 minutes.

3. Sprinkle with cheese and remaining onions. Bake until cheese is melted and a toothpick inserted into cornbread layer comes out clean, 3-5 minutes longer.

1 SERVING: 541 cal., 26g fat (9g sat. fat), 95mg chol., 1491mg sod., 48g carb. (14g sugars, 5g fiber), 28g pro.

SIMPLE SWAP
Feel free to substitute 1¾ cups fresh or frozen corn for the canned.

STOVETOP CHEESEBURGER PASTA

Cheeseburgers are delicious in any form, but I'm partial to this creamy pasta
dish that seriously tastes just like the real thing. It's weeknight comfort in a bowl.
—*Tracy Avis, Peterborough, ON*

TAKES: 30 MIN. • **MAKES:** 8 SERVINGS

1 pkg. (16 oz.) penne pasta
1 lb. ground beef
¼ cup butter, cubed
½ cup all-purpose flour
2 cups 2% milk
1¼ cups beef broth
1 Tbsp. Worcestershire sauce
3 tsp. ground mustard
2 cans (14½ oz. each)
    diced tomatoes, drained
4 green onions, chopped
3 cups shredded Colby-
    Monterey Jack cheese, divided
⅔ cup grated Parmesan cheese,
    divided

1. Cook pasta according to package directions; drain.

2. Meanwhile, in a Dutch oven, cook beef over medium heat until no longer pink, 5-7 minutes, breaking it into crumbles. Remove from pan with a slotted spoon; pour off drippings.

3. In same pan, melt butter over low heat; stir in flour until smooth. Cook and stir until lightly browned, 2-3 minutes (do not burn). Gradually whisk in milk, broth, Worcestershire sauce and mustard. Bring to a boil, stirring constantly; cook and stir until thickened, 1-2 minutes. Stir in tomatoes; return to a boil. Reduce heat; simmer, covered, 5 minutes.

4. Stir in green onions, pasta and beef; heat through. Stir in half the cheeses until melted. Sprinkle with remaining cheese; remove from heat. Let stand, covered, until cheeses are melted.

1½ CUPS: 616 cal., 29g fat (17g sat. fat), 98mg chol., 727mg sod., 56g carb. (7g sugars, 3g fiber), 33g pro.

GO GREEN

To add fun crunch and color, top the pasta with shredded iceberg lettuce just before serving. Feeling adventurous? Try topping it with sliced pickles too!

- BEEF -

MEXICAN BEEF COBBLER

*Add whatever you like—black beans, sour cream, even guacamole—to this
satisfying Mexican cobbler to make it your own!*
—Mary Brooks, Clay, MI

PREP: 20 MIN. • **BAKE:** 35 MIN. • **MAKES:** 6 SERVINGS

1. In a large skillet, cook the beef over medium heat until no longer pink, breaking it into crumbles; drain. Stir in the taco seasoning, salsa and corn; heat through. Transfer to an 11x7-in. baking dish; sprinkle with cheese.

2. In a small bowl, mix biscuit mix and milk just until blended; drop by tablespoonfuls over cheese. Sprinkle with pepper.

3. Bake, uncovered, at 350° for 35-45 minutes or until bubbly and topping is golden brown.

1 SERVING: 546 cal., 29g fat (13g sat. fat), 109mg chol., 1562mg sod., 37g carb. (8g sugars, 1g fiber), 32g pro.

1½ lbs. ground beef
1   envelope taco seasoning
1   jar (16 oz.) salsa
1   can (8¾ oz.) whole kernel
    corn, drained
2   cups shredded
    sharp cheddar cheese
1½ cups biscuit/baking mix
½   cup 2% milk
⅛   tsp. freshly ground pepper

*Save money by making your own
biscuit/baking mix. Recipe on p. 304.*

SOUTHWESTERN CASSEROLE

I've been making this mild family-pleasing casserole for years. It tastes wonderful and fits nicely into our budget. Best of all, the recipe makes a second casserole to freeze and enjoy later.
—*Joan Hallford, North Richland Hills, TX*

PREP: 25 MIN. · **BAKE:** 40 MIN. · **MAKES:** 2 CASSEROLES (6 SERVINGS EACH)

2 cups (8 oz.) uncooked
elbow macaroni
2 lbs. ground beef
1 large onion, chopped
2 garlic cloves, minced
2 cans (14½ oz. each)
diced tomatoes, undrained
1 can (16 oz.) kidney beans,
rinsed and drained
1 can (6 oz.) tomato paste
1 can (4 oz.) chopped
green chiles, drained
1½ tsp. salt
1 tsp. chili powder
½ tsp. ground cumin
¼ tsp. pepper
2 cups shredded
Monterey Jack cheese
2 jalapeno peppers,
seeded and chopped

1. Cook macaroni according to package directions. Meanwhile, in a large saucepan, cook beef and onion over medium heat until meat is no longer pink, breaking it into crumbles. Add garlic; cook 1 minute longer. Drain. Stir in next 8 ingredients. Bring to a boil. Reduce heat; simmer, uncovered, for 10 minutes. Drain macaroni; stir into beef mixture.

2. Preheat oven to 375°. Transfer macaroni mixture to 2 greased 2-qt. baking dishes. Top with cheese and jalapenos. Cover and bake for 30 minutes. Uncover; bake until bubbly and heated through, about 10 minutes longer. Serve 1 casserole. Cool the second; cover and freeze up to 3 months.

TO USE FROZEN CASSEROLE: Thaw in refrigerator 8 hours. Preheat oven to 375°. Remove from refrigerator 30 minutes before baking. Cover and bake, increasing time as necessary to heat through and for a thermometer inserted in center to read 165°, 20-25 minutes.

NOTE: Wear disposable gloves when cutting hot peppers; the oils can burn skin. Avoid touching your face.

1 CUP: 321 cal., 15g fat (7g sat. fat), 64mg chol., 673mg sod., 23g carb. (5g sugars, 4g fiber), 24g pro.

KOREAN BEEF & RICE

A friend raved about Korean bulgogi, which is beef cooked in soy sauce and ginger,
so I tried it. It's delicious! You'll dazzle the table with this tasty version of beef and rice.
—*Elizabeth King, Duluth, MN*

TAKES: 15 MIN. • **MAKES:** 4 SERVINGS

1. In a large skillet, cook beef and garlic over medium heat 6-8 minutes or until beef is no longer pink, breaking beef into crumbles. Meanwhile, in a small bowl, mix brown sugar, soy sauce, oil and seasonings.

2. Stir sauce into beef; heat through. Serve with rice. Sprinkle with green onions.

FREEZE OPTION: Freeze cooled meat mixture in freezer containers. To use, partially thaw in refrigerator overnight. Heat through in a saucepan, stirring occasionally.

½ CUP BEEF MIXTURE WITH ⅔ CUP RICE: 413 cal., 13g fat (4g sat. fat), 71mg chol., 647mg sod., 46g carb. (14g sugars, 3g fiber), 27g pro. **DIABETIC EXCHANGES:** 3 starch, 3 lean meat, ½ fat.

1   lb. lean ground beef (90% lean)
3   garlic cloves, minced
¼   cup packed brown sugar
¼   cup reduced-sodium soy sauce
2   tsp. sesame oil
¼   tsp. ground ginger
¼   tsp. crushed red pepper flakes
¼   tsp. pepper
2⅔ cups hot cooked brown rice
3   green onions, thinly sliced

MY TWO CENTS
"Very good! I added half a bag of coleslaw mix to the meat mixture and cooked it slightly. This added a little fiber and nutritional value while stretching the recipe a bit."

—KELLISCOTT, TASTEOFHOME.COM

TOURTIERE

When temperatures drop, people in our region start craving the ultimate
French Canadian comfort food—savory meat pie, also known as tourtiere.
—*Vivianne Remillard, St. Joseph, MB*

PREP: 25 MIN. • **BAKE:** 50 MIN. • **MAKES:** 6 SERVINGS

Dough for double-crust pie (9 in.)
1½ lbs. lean ground beef (90% lean)
1   lb. ground pork
1   medium onion, chopped
⅓   cup water
¾   tsp. salt
¾   tsp. ground cinnamon
¼   tsp. dried sage leaves
¼   tsp. ground cloves
¼   tsp. pepper
½   cup soft bread crumbs

1. On a lightly floured surface, roll half the dough to a ⅛-in.-thick circle. Line a 9-in. pie plate with crust; trim crust even with edge of plate. Set aside.

2. In a large skillet, cook the beef, pork and onion over medium heat until meat is no longer pink, breaking meat into crumbles; drain. Stir in water and seasonings, then bread crumbs.

3. Spoon into prepared crust. Roll out remaining dough to fit top of pie; place over filling. Trim, seal and flute edges. Cut slits in top.

4. Bake at 375° for 50-60 minutes or until crust is golden brown.

DOUGH FOR DOUBLE-CRUST PIE: Combine 2-½ cups all-purpose flour and ½ tsp. salt; cut in 1 cup cold butter until crumbly. Gradually add ⅓ to ⅔ cup ice water, tossing with a fork until dough holds together when pressed. Divide dough in half. Shape each into a disk; wrap and refrigerate 1 hour.

1 PIECE: 689 cal., 41g fat (16g sat. fat), 135mg chol., 687mg sod., 39g carb. (4g sugars, 1g fiber), 39g pro.

BAVARIAN POT ROAST

Since all my grandparents were German, it's no wonder that so many
Bavarian recipes have been handed down to me. In this classic European pot roast
recipe, the tang of tomato sauce and vinegar is balanced by cinnamon and ginger.
—*Susan Robertson, Hamilton, OH*

PREP: 15 MIN. • **COOK:** 2½ HOURS • **MAKES:** 10 SERVINGS

2 Tbsp. canola oil
1 boneless beef chuck roast (3 lbs.)
1¼ cups water
¾ cup beer or beef broth
1 can (8 oz.) tomato sauce
½ cup chopped onion
2 Tbsp. sugar
1 Tbsp. white vinegar
2 tsp. salt
1 tsp. ground cinnamon
1 bay leaf
½ tsp. pepper
½ tsp. ground ginger

1. In a Dutch oven, heat oil. Brown roast on all sides. Meanwhile, combine water, beer, tomato sauce, onion, sugar, vinegar, salt, cinnamon, bay leaf, pepper and ginger. Pour over meat and bring to a boil. Reduce heat; cover and simmer until meat is tender, 2½-3 hours.

2. Remove meat and slice. Discard bay leaf. If desired, thicken pan juices for gravy.

FREEZE OPTION: Place sliced pot roast in freezer containers; top with cooking juices. Cool and freeze. To use, partially thaw in refrigerator overnight. Microwave, covered, on high in a microwave-safe dish until heated through, stirring occasionally; add a little broth if necessary.

4 OZ. COOKED BEEF: 281 cal., 16g fat (5g sat. fat), 88mg chol., 633mg sod., 5g carb. (4g sugars, 0 fiber), 27g pro.

GARLIC SPAGHETTI SQUASH WITH MEAT SAUCE

*I have reduced grains and other starches in my diet due to health reasons,
so I was looking for satisfying meals that don't use pasta or potatoes. When I was tinkering
with this recipe, I discovered that spaghetti squash is fun to experiment with and eat.*
—*Becky Ruff, McGregor, IA*

PREP: 15 MIN. • **BAKE:** 45 MIN. • **MAKES:** 4 SERVINGS

1. Preheat oven to 375°. Cut squash lengthwise in half; remove and discard seeds. Place squash in a 13x9-in. baking pan, cut side down; add ½ in. hot water. Bake, uncovered, 40 minutes. Drain water from pan; turn squash cut side up. Bake until squash is tender, 5-10 minutes longer.

2. Meanwhile, in a large skillet, cook beef and mushrooms over medium heat until beef is no longer pink, 6-8 minutes, breaking up beef into crumbles; drain. Add half the garlic; cook and stir 1 minute. Stir in tomatoes, pasta sauce and ¼ tsp. pepper; bring to a boil. Reduce heat; simmer, uncovered, 15-20 minutes.

3. When squash is cool enough to handle, use a fork to separate strands. In a large skillet, heat oil over medium heat. Add remaining garlic; cook and stir 1 minute. Stir in squash, salt and remaining pepper; heat through. Serve with meat sauce and, if desired, cheese.

1   medium spaghetti squash
    (about 4 lbs.)
1   lb. lean ground beef (90% lean)
2   cups sliced fresh mushrooms
4   garlic cloves, minced, divided
4   plum tomatoes, chopped
2   cups pasta sauce
½   tsp. pepper, divided
1   Tbsp. olive oil
¼   tsp. salt
    Grated Parmesan cheese,
    optional

**Save money by making your own
marinara sauce. Recipe on p. 313.*

1¼ CUPS SQUASH WITH 1 CUP MEAT SAUCE: 354 cal., 15g fat (4g sat. fat), 71mg chol., 727mg sod., 30g carb. (17g sugars, 7g fiber), 27g pro. **DIABETIC EXCHANGES:** 3 lean meat, 2 starch, 1 fat.

- BEEF -

TACOS IN A BOWL

This easy skillet dish offers a tasty use for leftover taco meat.
Garnish it with sour cream and salsa for added southwestern flavor.
—*Sue Schoening, Sheboygan, WI*

TAKES: 25 MIN. • **MAKES:** 2 SERVINGS

1. In a small skillet, cook beef and onion over medium heat until meat is no longer pink, breaking beef into crumbles; drain. Stir in the tomatoes, taco seasoning and water. Bring to a boil. Add ramen noodles (discard seasoning packet or save for another use). Cook and stir until noodles are tender, 3-5 minutes.

2. Spoon into serving bowls; sprinkle with cheese and, if desired, tortilla chips.

1 CUP: 480 cal., 21g fat (10g sat. fat), 85mg chol., 1279mg sod., 40g carb. (3g sugars, 2g fiber), 30g pro.

½ lb. lean ground beef (90% lean)
2 Tbsp. finely chopped onion
¾ cup canned diced tomatoes, drained
2 Tbsp. taco seasoning
1 cup water
1 pkg. (3 oz.) ramen noodles
¼ cup shredded cheddar or Mexican cheese blend
   Crushed tortilla chips, optional

BEEFY CHILI DOGS

For years people have told me I make the best hot dog chili out there. It's timeless and family-friendly, and I usually carry the recipe with me because people ask for it.
—*Vicki Boyd, Mechanicsville, VA*

TAKES: 30 MIN. • **MAKES:** 8 SERVINGS (2 CUPS CHILI)

1 lb. ground beef
1 tsp. chili powder
½ tsp. garlic powder
½ tsp. paprika
¼ tsp. cayenne pepper
1 cup ketchup
8 hot dogs
8 hot dog buns, split
Optional: Shredded cheddar cheese and chopped onion

1. For chili, in a large skillet, cook beef over medium heat 5-7 minutes or until no longer pink, breaking into crumbles; drain. Transfer beef to a food processor; pulse until finely chopped.

2. Return beef to skillet; stir in the seasonings and ketchup. Bring to a boil. Reduce heat; simmer, covered, 15-20 minutes to allow the flavors to blend, stirring occasionally.

3. Meanwhile, cook hot dogs according to package directions. Serve in buns with chili. If desired, top with cheese and onion.

FREEZE OPTION: Freeze cooled chili in a freezer container. To use, partially thaw in refrigerator overnight. Heat through in a saucepan, stirring occasionally; add water if necessary.

1 HOT DOG WITH ¼ CUP CHILI: 400 cal., 22g fat (9g sat fat), 60mg chol., 1092mg sod., 31g carb. (11g sugars, 1g fiber), 19g pro.

SOMBRERO PASTA SALAD

I take this slightly spicy salad to almost every party or picnic I attend.
Every time I come home with lots of compliments, but never any leftovers!
—Patty Ehlen, Burlington, WI

PREP: 30 MIN. + CHILLING • **MAKES:** 10 SERVINGS

---

1 pkg. (16 oz.) spiral pasta
1 lb. ground beef
¾ cup water
1 envelope taco seasoning
2 cups shredded cheddar cheese
1 large green pepper, chopped
1 medium onion, chopped
1 medium tomato, chopped
2 cans (2¼ oz. each)
   sliced ripe olives, drained
1 bottle (16 oz.) Catalina or
   Western salad dressing

1. Cook pasta according to package directions. Meanwhile, in a skillet, cook beef over medium heat until no longer pink, breaking meat into crumbles; drain. Add water and taco seasoning; simmer, uncovered, for 15 minutes.

2. Rinse pasta in cold water and drain; place in a large bowl. Add beef mixture, cheese, green pepper, onion, tomato and olives; mix well. Add the dressing and toss to coat.

3. Cover and refrigerate for at least 1 hour.

NOTE: If you'll be refrigerating this pasta salad for more than 1 hour, reserve ½ cup dressing to stir into the salad just before serving.

1 SERVING: 548 cal., 29g fat (9g sat. fat), 46mg chol., 941mg sod., 53g carb. (14g sugars, 2g fiber), 19g pro.

- BEEF -

CABBAGE ROLL CASSEROLE

I layer cabbage with tomato sauce and beef to create a hearty
casserole that tastes like cabbage rolls—but without all the work.
—*Doreen Martin, Kitimat, BC*

PREP: 20 MIN. • **BAKE:** 55 MIN. • **MAKES:** 12 SERVINGS

1. Preheat oven to 375°. In a large skillet, cook beef and onion over medium heat until meat is no longer pink, breaking beef into crumbles. Add garlic; cook 1 minute longer. Drain. Stir in 1 can tomato sauce and next 6 ingredients. Bring to a boil. Reduce heat; simmer, covered, 5 minutes. Stir in rice and bacon; remove from heat.

2. Layer a third of the cabbage in a greased 13x9-in. baking dish. Top with half the meat mixture. Repeat layers; top with remaining cabbage. Pour remaining tomato sauce over top.

3. Cover and bake 45 minutes. Uncover; sprinkle with cheese. Bake until cheese is melted, about 10 minutes. Let stand 5 minutes before serving. If desired, sprinkle with coarsely ground pepper.

1 PIECE: 256 cal., 13g fat (5g sat. fat), 56mg chol., 544mg sod., 17g carb. (4g sugars, 3g fiber), 20g pro.

2   lbs. ground beef
1   large onion, chopped
3   garlic cloves, minced
2   cans (15 oz. each)
    tomato sauce, divided
1   tsp. dried thyme
½   tsp. dill weed
½   tsp. rubbed sage
¼   tsp. salt
¼   tsp. pepper
¼   tsp. cayenne pepper
2   cups cooked rice
4   bacon strips, cooked
    and crumbled
1   medium head cabbage
    (2 lbs.), shredded
1   cup shredded part-skim
    mozzarella cheese
    Coarsely ground pepper, optional

MY TWO CENTS
"I enjoy making this since it is SO MUCH easier than making traditional cabbage rolls. Everything is layered in one dish!"
—ALLYBILLHORN, TASTEOFHOME.COM

MELT-IN-YOUR-MOUTH MEAT LOAF

When my husband and I were first married, he refused to eat meat loaf because he said it was bland and dry. Then I prepared this version, and it became his favorite meal.
—Suzanne Codner, Starbuck, MN

PREP: 15 MIN. • **COOK:** 5¼ HOURS + STANDING • **MAKES:** 6 SERVINGS

2 large eggs
¾ cup 2% milk
⅔ cup seasoned bread crumbs
2 tsp. dried minced onion
1 tsp. salt
½ tsp. rubbed sage
1½ lbs. ground beef
¼ cup ketchup
2 Tbsp. brown sugar
1 tsp. ground mustard
½ tsp. Worcestershire sauce

1. Cut two 25x3-in. strips of heavy-duty foil; crisscross so they resemble an X. Place strips on bottom and up sides of a 5-qt. slow cooker. Coat the strips with cooking spray.

2. Combine the first 6 ingredients. Crumble beef over mixture and mix lightly but thoroughly. Shape into a round loaf; place in center of strips in slow cooker. Cook, covered, on low 5-6 hours or until a thermometer reads at least 160°.

3. In a small bowl, whisk ketchup, brown sugar, mustard and Worcestershire sauce. Spoon over meat loaf. Cook until heated through, about 15 minutes longer. Using foil strips as handles, remove meat loaf to a platter. Let stand 10-15 minutes before slicing.

1 PIECE: 346 cal., 17g fat (7g sat. fat), 150mg chol., 800mg sod., 18g carb. (8g sugars, 1g fiber), 28g pro.

THRIFTY TIP

You can use dried minced onion and freshly chopped onion interchangeably in casseroles, soups, meat loaves and other cooked dishes: 1 Tbsp. dried minced onion equals 4 Tbsp. minced raw onion. So, for this recipe you could sub in a scant 3 Tbsp. fresh onion if you don't have dried.

TERIYAKI BURGERS

The teriyaki sauce takes these cheeseburgers from ordinary to oh boy!
Look for this sauce in the Chinese food section of your grocery store.
—*Rose Thusfield, Holocombe, WI*

TAKES: 30 MIN. • **MAKES:** 4 SERVINGS

2 medium onions, sliced
½ cup reduced-sodium
    teriyaki sauce
1 lb. lean ground beef (90% lean)
4 slices part-skim mozzarella
    cheese or provolone cheese
    Hamburger buns

1. In a large skillet, saute onions in teriyaki sauce until tender. Shape ground beef into 4 patties; place on top of onions and cook for 4-6 minutes on each side or until a thermometer reads 160° and juices run clear.

2. Top each burger with cheese and onions. Serve on buns.

1 SERVING: 308 cal., 13g fat (6g sat. fat), 71mg chol., 1446mg sod., 12g carb. (9g sugars, 2g fiber), 32g pro.

EASY CUBAN PICADILLO

My girlfriend gave me this delicious recipe years ago. I've made it ever since for family and friends.
My daughter says it's the best dish I make and loves to take leftovers to school for lunch the next day.
—*Mario Wiolgus, Wayne, NJ*

TAKES: 25 MIN. • **MAKES:** 4 SERVINGS

1. In a large skillet, cook beef with pepper and onion over medium-high heat until no longer pink, 5-7 minutes; crumble beef. Stir in tomato sauce, olives, raisins and vinegar; bring to a boil. Reduce heat; simmer, uncovered, until raisins are softened, 5-6 minutes.

2. Serve with rice. If desired, top with fresh cilantro to serve.

1 CUP BEEF MIXTURE WITH ½ CUP RICE: 363 cal., 13g fat (4g sat. fat), 71mg chol., 683mg sod., 36g carb. (7g sugars, 2g fiber), 26g pro. **DIABETIC EXCHANGES:** 3 lean meat, 2½ starch, 1 fat.

1 lb. lean ground beef (90% lean)
1 small green pepper, chopped
¼ cup chopped onion
1 can (8 oz.) tomato sauce
½ cup sliced pimiento-
   stuffed olives
¼ cup raisins
1 Tbsp. cider vinegar
2 cups hot cooked rice
   Fresh cilantro leaves, optional

MY TWO CENTS
"Simple and delicious. I did add garlic. I also used golden raisins vs. traditional because we like them better. They are a tad more expensive but worth it."

—KATIE HAUER, TASTEOFHOME.COM

EASY FRY BREAD TACOS

My niece gave me this hearty recipe. Frozen bread dough makes the tacos easy to prep.
—Robin Wells, Tulsa, Oklahoma

PREP: 10 MIN. + RISING • **COOK:** 45 MIN. • **MAKES:** 12 SERVINGS

1 loaf frozen white bread
  dough, thawed

TOPPING:
1 lb. ground beef
1 lb. hot bulk pork sausage
1 envelope taco seasoning
1 can (15 oz.) pinto beans,
  rinsed and drained
½ cup water
  Oil for deep-fat frying
  Optional toppings: Chopped
  tomato, finely chopped onion,
  shredded lettuce, shredded
  cheddar cheese and taco sauce

1. Allow dough to rise according to package directions. Meanwhile, for topping, cook beef and sausage in a skillet over medium heat until no longer pink, breaking meat into crumbles; drain. Stir in taco seasoning, beans and water. Simmer for 15-20 minutes or until the water is almost evaporated; set aside.

2. After dough rises, punch down. Divide dough into 12 equal balls. Using a small amount of flour, roll each ball into a 6-in. circle (dough will be thin).

3. In an electric skillet or deep fryer, heat 1 in. oil to 350°. Gently place 1 dough circle into oil. Fry until golden brown, 1-2 minutes, turning once. Drain tortillas on paper towels; keep warm. Serve with optional toppings of your choice.

1 TACO: 373 cal., 22g fat (5g sat. fat), 44mg chol., 777mg sod., 27g carb. (2g sugars, 3g fiber), 16g pro.

PIZZA MACARONI BAKE

What do you get when you combine macaroni and cheese with pizza fixings?
This hearty, family-pleasing casserole! It's so easy and so tasty.
—*Nancy Porterfield, Gap Mills, WV*

PREP: 30 MIN. • **BAKE:** 20 MIN. • **MAKES:** 8 SERVINGS

1. Set the cheese packet from the dinner mix aside. In a saucepan, bring water to a boil. Add macaroni; cook for 8-10 minutes or until tender.

2. Meanwhile, in a large skillet, cook the beef, onion and green pepper over medium heat until meat is no longer pink, breaking beef into crumbles; drain. Drain macaroni; stir in the contents of cheese packet.

3. Transfer to a greased 13x9-in. baking dish. Sprinkle with cheddar cheese. Top with the beef mixture, pizza sauce, pepperoni and mozzarella cheese.

4. Bake, uncovered, at 350° until heated through, 20-25 minutes.

1 SERVING: 376 cal., 20g fat (9g sat. fat), 64mg chol., 827mg sod., 13g carb. (6g sugars, 2g fiber), 23g pro.

1 pkg. (7¼ oz.) macaroni and cheese dinner mix
6 cups water
1 lb. ground beef
1 medium onion, chopped
1 small green pepper, chopped
1 cup shredded cheddar cheese
1 jar (14 oz.) pizza sauce
1 pkg. (3½ oz.) sliced pepperoni
1 cup shredded part-skim mozzarella cheese

SO-EASY SLOPPY JOES

Everybody in the family will love the zesty flavor of this yummy comfort food.
Try it spooned over warmed cornbread if you don't have buns.
—*Karen Anderson, Cuyahoga Falls, OH*

TAKES: 30 MIN. • **MAKES:** 6 SERVINGS

In a large skillet, cook beef over medium heat until no longer pink, 5-7 minutes, breaking meat into crumbles; drain. Stir in the tomatoes, tomato paste, ketchup, brown sugar, mustard and salt. Bring to a boil. Reduce heat; simmer, uncovered, for 5 minutes. Serve on buns with arugula if desired.

FREEZE OPTION: Freeze cooled meat mixture in freezer containers. To use, partially thaw in refrigerator overnight. Heat through in a saucepan, stirring occasionally; add a little water if necessary.

1 SERVING: 478 cal., 18g fat (6g sat. fat), 70mg chol., 918mg sod., 49g carb. (15g sugars, 2g fiber), 30g pro.

1½ lbs. ground beef
1 can (10 oz.) diced tomatoes and green chiles, undrained
1 can (6 oz.) tomato paste
¼ cup ketchup
2 Tbsp. brown sugar
1 Tbsp. spicy brown mustard
¼ tsp. salt
6 sandwich buns, split
  Fresh arugula, optional

DELUXE CHEESEBURGER SALAD

I was planning to grill burgers, and then it dawned on me:
How about a cheeseburger salad? Tomato adds a fresh flavor boost.
—Pam Jefferies, Cantrall, IL

TAKES: 30 MIN. • **MAKES:** 4 SERVINGS

1 lb. ground beef
2 tsp. Montreal steak seasoning
6 cups torn iceberg lettuce
2 cups shredded cheddar cheese
1 cup salad croutons
1 medium tomato, chopped
1 small onion, halved
  and thinly sliced
½ cup dill pickle slices
  Thousand Island salad dressing

1. In a large bowl, combine beef and steak seasoning, mixing lightly but thoroughly. Shape into twenty ½-in.-thick patties. Grill mini burgers, covered, over medium heat, 3-4 minutes on each side or until a thermometer reads 160°.

2. In a large bowl, combine lettuce, mini burgers, cheese, croutons, tomato, onion and pickles. Serve with salad dressing.

FREEZE OPTION: Place patties on a waxed paper-lined baking sheet; cover and freeze until firm. Remove from sheet and transfer to an airtight container; return to freezer. To use, cook frozen patties as directed, increasing time as necessary for a thermometer to read 160°.

1 SERVING: 511 cal., 34g fat (17g sat. fat), 128mg chol., 1033mg sod., 14g carb. (4g sugars, 3g fiber), 36g pro.

MAKE IT YOUR OWN

Swap in another shredded cheese, such as Monterey Jack, sharp cheddar or Swiss. Instead of croutons, toss in some freshly baked shoestring french fries or miniature Tater Tots. Leftover bacon is a winner here too. Just sprinkle chopped bacon over the top for a bacon cheeseburger salad.

FREEZER BURRITOS

I love burritos, but the frozen ones are high in salt and chemicals. So I created these. They're wonderful to have on hand for quick dinners or late-night snacks—I've even had them for breakfast!
—*Laura Winemiller, Delta, PA*

PREP: 35 MIN. • **COOK:** 15 MIN. • **MAKES:** 12 SERVINGS

1. In a large skillet, cook beef and onion over medium heat until meat is no longer pink, 5-7 minutes, breaking meat into crumbles; drain. Stir in salsa and taco seasoning. Bring to a boil. Reduce heat; simmer, uncovered, for 2-3 minutes. Transfer to a large bowl; set aside.

2. In a food processor, combine pinto beans and water. Cover and process until almost smooth. Add to beef mixture. Stir in cheese.

3. Spoon ½ cup beef mixture down the center of each tortilla. Fold ends and sides over filling; roll up. Wrap each burrito in waxed paper and foil. Freeze for up to 1 month.

TO USE FROZEN BURRITOS: Remove foil and waxed paper. Place 1 burrito on a microwave-safe plate. Microwave on high until a thermometer reads 165°, 2½-2¾ minutes, turning burrito over once. Let stand for 20 seconds.

1 BURRITO: 345 cal., 11g fat (4g sat. fat), 36mg chol., 677mg sod., 40g carb. (3g sugars, 3g fiber), 22g pro. **DIABETIC EXCHANGES:** 2½ starch, 2 lean meat, ½ fat.

1¼ lbs. lean ground beef (90% lean)
¼ cup finely chopped onion
1¼ cups salsa
2 Tbsp. reduced-sodium taco seasoning
2 cans (15 oz. each) pinto beans, rinsed and drained
½ cup water
2 cups shredded reduced-fat cheddar cheese
12 flour tortillas (8 in.), warmed

BEEF MACARONI SKILLET

This stovetop favorite is tasty and stick-to-your-ribs.
It's easy to prepare—perfect after a long day at work.
—*Carmen Edwards, Midland, TX*

PREP: 15 MIN. • **COOK:** 20 MIN. • **MAKES:** 2 SERVINGS

½ lb. lean ground beef (90% lean)
⅓ cup chopped onion
¼ cup chopped green pepper
1½ cups spicy hot V8 juice
½ cup uncooked elbow macaroni
1 tsp. Worcestershire sauce
¼ tsp. pepper

In a large skillet, cook the beef, onion and green pepper over medium heat until meat is no longer pink, breaking meat into crumbles; drain. Stir in the remaining ingredients. Bring to a boil. Reduce heat; cover and simmer for 18-20 minutes or until macaroni is tender.

1¼ CUPS: 291 cal., 9g fat (4g sat. fat), 56mg chol., 689mg sod., 25g carb. (8g sugars, 2g fiber), 26g pro. **DIABETIC EXCHANGES:** 3 lean meat, 2 vegetable, 1 starch.

MY TWO CENTS
"I love this recipe. It doubles well in order to use a 1-lb. package of beef. The last time I made it, I didn't have any green pepper. I used celery and carrot instead, and it was delicious."
—KRISTIRACINES, TASTEOFHOME.COM

- BEEF -

ONE-POT STUFFED PEPPER DINNER

Thick like chili and with plenty of stuffed pepper flavor, this dish will warm you up on chilly days.
—*Charlotte Smith, McDonald, PA*

TAKES: 30 MIN. • **MAKES:** 4 SERVINGS

1   lb. lean ground beef (90% lean)
3   medium green peppers, chopped (about 3 cups)
3   garlic cloves, minced
2   cans (14½ oz. each) Italian diced tomatoes, undrained
2   cups water
1   can (6 oz.) tomato paste
2   Tbsp. shredded Parmesan cheese
¼   tsp. pepper
1   cup uncooked instant rice
    Additional Parmesan cheese, optional

1. In a Dutch oven, cook and crumble beef with green peppers and garlic over medium-high heat until the meat is no longer pink and peppers are tender, 5-7 minutes; drain.

2. Stir in tomatoes, water, tomato paste, cheese and pepper; bring to a boil. Stir in rice; remove from heat. Let stand, covered, 5 minutes. If desired, sprinkle with additional cheese.

2 CUPS: 415 cal., 10g fat (4g sat. fat), 72mg chol., 790mg sod., 51g carb. (20g sugars, 5g fiber), 30g pro.

MY FAVORITE BURGER

After having a burger similar to this at a diner years ago, I tried to lighten it up
without losing the amazing flavors. Now I can enjoy a burger more often without feeling guilty!
—Kris Swihart, Perrysburg, OH

PREP: 25 MIN. • **GRILL:** 15 MIN. • **MAKES:** 4 SERVINGS

¼ cup grated onion
½ tsp. garlic powder
¼ tsp. salt
¼ tsp. pepper
1 lb. lean ground beef (90% lean)
1 cup sliced fresh mushrooms
½ cup sliced sweet onion
4 kaiser rolls, split
4 oz. fat-free cream cheese
2 bacon strips, cooked
   and crumbled

1. In a large bowl, combine the onion, garlic powder, salt and pepper. Crumble beef over mixture and mix well. Shape into 4 patties.

2. Grill patties, covered, on oiled rack over medium heat or broil 4 in. from the heat for 4-6 minutes on each side or until a thermometer reads 160°.

3. Meanwhile, in a small skillet coated with cooking spray, cook and stir the mushrooms and onion over medium heat until onion is golden brown. Grill rolls for 1-2 minutes or until lightly toasted.

4. Spread rolls with cream cheese; top with burgers and mushroom mixture. Sprinkle with bacon.

1 SERVING: 410 cal., 13g fat (5g sat. fat), 75mg chol., 737mg sod., 37g carb. (4g sugars, 2g fiber), 33g pro.

PATRIOTIC TACO SALAD

When my daughter asked to have a patriotic theme for her July birthday party, I made this refreshing dish.
If you want to prepare your salad in advance, omit the layer of chips and serve them on the side.
—*Glenda Jarboek, Oroville, CA*

PREP: 20 MIN. • **COOK:** 20 MIN. • **MAKES:** 8 SERVINGS

1. In a large skillet, cook beef and onion over medium heat until meat is no longer pink, breaking it into crumbles; drain. Stir in the water, tomato paste and taco seasoning. Bring to a boil. Reduce heat; simmer, uncovered, for 20 minutes.

2. Place chips in an ungreased 13x9-in. dish. Spread beef mixture evenly over the top. Cover with lettuce. Place olives in upper left corner to represent stars. To form stripes, add cheese and tomatoes in alternating rows. Serve immediately.

1 CUP: 357 cal., 20g fat (9g sat. fat), 63mg chol., 747mg sod., 24g carb. (4g sugars, 2g fiber), 20g pro.

1   lb. ground beef
1   medium onion, chopped
1½ cups water
1   can (6 oz.) tomato paste
1   envelope taco seasoning
6   cups tortilla or corn chips
4   to 5 cups shredded lettuce
9   to 10 pitted large olives,
    sliced lengthwise
2   cups shredded cheddar cheese
2   cups cherry tomatoes, halved

CHICKEN-FRIED CHOPS

It takes only a few minutes to brown the meat before assembling this savory meal.
The pork chops simmer all day in a flavorful sauce until they're tender.
—*Connie Slocum, Brunswick, GA*

PREP: 15 MIN. • **COOK:** 6 HOURS • **MAKES:** 6 SERVINGS

½ cup all-purpose flour
2 tsp. salt
1½ tsp. ground mustard
½ tsp. garlic powder
6 pork loin chops (¾ in. thick), trimmed
2 Tbsp. canola oil
1 can (10¾ oz.) condensed cream of chicken soup, undiluted
⅓ cup water

In a shallow bowl, combine flour, salt, mustard and garlic powder; add pork chops and turn to coat. In a large skillet, heat oil over medium-high heat; brown meat on both sides in batches. Place in a 5-qt. slow cooker. Combine soup and water; pour over chops. Cover and cook on low until meat is tender, 6-8 hours. If desired, thicken pan juices and serve with the pork chops.

1 PORK CHOP: 453 cal., 27g fat (9g sat. fat), 115mg chol., 1232mg sod., 13g carb. (0 sugars, 1g fiber), 38g pro.

MY TWO CENTS
*"These were tender
and tasty. The gravy
was so good over
mashed potatoes!"*
—GUNSLINGER, TASTEOFHOME.COM

BRATS WITH SAUERKRAUT

I've made many variations of this excellent main dish. It would be popular at a party or potluck. The bratwurst can be plain, smoked or cheese-flavored and served whole or cut in slices, with a bun or without.
—*Darlene Dixon, Hanover, MN*

PREP: 10 MIN. • **COOK:** 6 HOURS • **MAKES:** 8 SERVINGS

1. Place the bratwurst in a 5-qt. slow cooker. In a large bowl, combine the sauerkraut, apples, bacon, brown sugar, onion and mustard; spoon over the bratwurst.

2. Cover and cook on low until a thermometer inserted in the sausage reads 160°, 6-8 hours.

3. Place brats in buns; using a slotted spoon, top with sauerkraut mixture.

1 BRAT: 534 cal., 28g fat (11g sat. fat), 53mg chol., 1188mg sod., 51g carb. (18g sugars, 4g fiber), 21g pro.

8   uncooked bratwurst links
1   can (14 oz.) sauerkraut, rinsed and well drained
2   medium apples, peeled and finely chopped
3   bacon strips, cooked and crumbled
¼   cup packed brown sugar
¼   cup finely chopped onion
1   tsp. ground mustard
8   brat buns, split

GRILLED MANGO-GLAZED HAM

I'm always looking for new ways to prepare ham, but many of my cookbooks
have the same old tried-and-true glazes. When I tasted this one, I knew I had hit the jackpot!
—Sandy Lewis, Appleton, WI

PREP: 30 MIN. • **GRILL:** 25 MIN. • **MAKES:** 8 SERVINGS

1½ cups red wine vinegar
½ cup sugar
1 tsp. finely chopped
   jalapeno pepper
1 tsp. minced fresh gingerroot
1 medium ripe mango or
   2 medium ripe peaches,
   peeled and cut into wedges
1 fully cooked boneless
   ham steak (about 2 lbs.)
⅛ tsp. pepper

1. In a small saucepan, combine the vinegar, sugar, jalapeno and ginger. Bring to a boil. Reduce heat; simmer, uncovered, for 25-30 minutes or until glaze is thick and caramelized. Strain and cool. Place mango in a food processor or blender; cover and process until smooth. Stir into glaze; set aside.

2. Sprinkle both sides of ham steak with pepper. Grill ham on an oiled rack, covered, over medium heat for 10 minutes on each side or until heated through. Brush both sides of ham with mango glaze; grill 5 minutes longer. Serve with remaining glaze.

NOTE: Wear disposable gloves when cutting hot peppers; the oils can burn skin. Avoid touching your face.

4 OZ. COOKED HAM WITH 2 TBSP. GLAZE: 207 cal., 4g fat (1g sat. fat), 58mg chol., 1178mg sod., 22g carb. (18g sugars, 1g fiber), 21g pro.

SIMPLE SWAP

Crystallized ginger is a good emergency stand-in when you don't have fresh ginger for your recipes. Just soak a few slices of ginger in hot water to soften them and remove excess sugar, then chop and use. Use about triple the amount of crystallized ginger in place of fresh.

THE BEST SAUSAGE PIZZAS

What makes this recipe unique is the slow overnight fermentation of the dough.
The flour has time to hydrate and relax, which makes the dough so much easier to roll out!
—*Josh Rink, Milwaukee, WI*

PREP: 30 MIN. · **BAKE:** 15 MIN. · **MAKES:** 2 PIZZAS (8 PIECES EACH)

2 lbs. pizza dough
1 lb. bulk Italian sausage
1 cup pizza sauce
4 cups shredded part-skim
   mozzarella cheese
1 medium red onion, sliced
1 medium green pepper, chopped
2 cups sliced fresh mushrooms
   Optional: Grated Parmesan
   cheese, crushed red pepper
   flakes and fresh oregano leaves

**Save money by making your own
pizza dough. Recipe on p. 316.*

1. Divide dough in half. With greased fingers, pat each half onto an ungreased 12-in. pizza pan. Prick dough thoroughly with a fork. Bake at 400° until lightly browned, 10-12 minutes. Meanwhile, in a large skillet, cook the sausage over medium heat until no longer pink, breaking it into crumbles; drain.

2. Spread pizza sauce over crusts. Top with cheese, onion, green pepper, mushrooms and sausage. Bake at 400° until golden brown and cheese is bubbling, 12-15 minutes. If desired, top with grated Parmesan cheese, crushed red pepper flakes and fresh oregano leaves.

FREEZE OPTION: Wrap unbaked pizzas and freeze for up to 2 months. To use, unwrap and place on pizza pans; thaw in the refrigerator. Bake at 400° until crust is golden brown, 18-22 minutes.

1 PIECE: 344 cal., 20g fat (7g sat. fat), 41mg chol., 651mg sod., 26g carb. (2g sugars, 1g fiber), 15g pro.

PORK LO MEIN

My husband teases me about using him as a guinea pig in the kitchen. But he's always an eager participant whenever I present attractive, tasty meals like this at dinnertime.
—*Billie Bethel, Waynesville, NC*

TAKES: 20 MIN. • **MAKES:** 4 SERVINGS

1   lb. ground pork
1   cup thinly sliced carrots
1   cup chopped onion
1   garlic clove, minced
2   pkg. (3 oz. each) soy sauce
    or chicken ramen noodles
1½ cups water
1   cup frozen peas
6   cups shredded romaine

1. In a large skillet coated with cooking spray, cook pork, carrots, onion and garlic over medium heat until pork is no longer pink, breaking it into crumbles; drain.

2. Break noodles into skillet, stir in seasoning packets. Stir in water and peas. Bring to a boil; reduce heat and simmer for 6-8 minutes or until noodles and vegetables are tender, stirring several times. Add the romaine; heat and stir until wilted.

1 CUP: 398 cal., 20g fat (8g sat. fat), 76mg chol., 570mg sod., 28g carb. (8g sugars, 5g fiber), 27g pro.

MY TWO CENTS
"My family is made up of picky eaters. This is one of the easiest and most delicious meals. I never have leftovers. This is a must-try."
—LOUJON, TASTEOFHOME.COM

ALL-DAY HAM HOCKS & BEANS

My family loves New Orleans-style cooking, so I make this dish often.
I appreciate how simple it is, and the smoky ham flavor is scrumptious.
—Celinda Dahlgren, Napa, CA

PREP: 20 MIN. + SOAKING • **COOK:** 8½ HOURS • **MAKES:** 6 SERVINGS

1. Sort beans and rinse in cold water. Place beans in a 3-qt. slow cooker. Add 4 cups water; cover and let stand overnight.

2. Drain and rinse beans, discarding liquid. Return beans to slow cooker; add ham hocks, onion, garlic, cumin and 3 cups water. Cover and cook on low for 8-10 hours or until beans are tender.

3. Remove ham hocks; cool slightly. Remove meat from bones. Finely chop meat and return to slow cooker; discard bones. Stir in the tomato, pepper and salt; cover and cook on high for 30 minutes or until pepper is tender. Serve with rice.

FREEZE OPTION: Freeze cooled bean mixture in freezer containers. To use, partially thaw in refrigerator overnight. Microwave, covered, on high in a microwave-safe dish until heated through, stirring occasionally; add a little water if necessary

1 cup dried red beans
2 smoked ham hocks
1 medium onion, chopped
1½ tsp. minced garlic
1 tsp. ground cumin
3 cups water
1 medium tomato, chopped
1 medium green pepper, chopped
1 tsp. salt
4 cups hot cooked rice

⅔ CUP BEAN MIXTURE WITH ⅔ CUP RICE: 297 cal., 7g fat (3g sat. fat), 33mg chol., 441mg sod., 50g carb. (3g sugars, 12g fiber), 17g pro

GREAT PORK CHOP BAKE

A friend brought this hearty meat-and-potatoes bake to our home when I returned
from the hospital with our youngest child. Since then, we have enjoyed the recipe many
times. It's a snap to throw together on a busy day, then pop into the oven to bake.
The tender chops, potato wedges and golden gravy are simple and satisfying.
—*Rosie Glenn, Los Alamos, NM*

PREP: 10 MIN. • **BAKE:** 50 MIN. • **MAKES:** 6 SERVINGS

1   can (10¾ oz.) condensed
    cream of chicken soup, undiluted
3   Tbsp. ketchup
2   Tbsp. Worcestershire sauce
½   tsp. salt
¼   tsp. pepper
4   medium potatoes,
    cut into ½-in. wedges
1   medium onion, sliced into rings
6   bone-in pork loin chops
    (¾ in. thick and 8 oz. each)
1   Tbsp. canola oil

1. In a large bowl, combine the soup, ketchup, Worcestershire sauce, salt and
pepper. Add potatoes and onion; toss to coat. Transfer to a greased 13x9-in.
baking dish. Cover and bake at 350° for 40 minutes.

2. Meanwhile, in a large skillet, brown pork chops in oil. Place chops on top
of potatoes and onions. Bake, covered, until a thermometer reads 145° and
potatoes are tender, 10-15 minutes longer.

1 SERVING: 520 cal., 24g fat (8g sat. fat), 115mg chol., 801mg sod., 34g carb.
(5g sugars, 4g fiber), 40g pro.

TIMESAVING TECHNIQUE

Cut potato wedges fast
with an apple slicer.
First, cut a thin slice off
the end of the potato for
stability. Stand potato
upright, place the slicer
on top and gently push
down. Presto!

HOT DOG CASSEROLE

When our children were small and I was busy trying to get done all those extra things
that are part of a mom's normal schedule, I would make this quick hot dish. Kids love it!
—JoAnn Gunio, Franklin, NC

PREP: 20 MIN. • **BAKE:** 70 MIN. • **MAKES:** 8 SERVINGS

1. Preheat oven to 350°. In a small saucepan, melt butter. Stir in flour, salt and pepper until smooth. Gradually add milk. Bring to a boil; cook and stir until thickened and bubbly, about 2 minutes.

2. In a greased 2½-qt. baking dish, layer with a third of the potatoes, half the hot dogs and half the onion. Repeat layers. Top with remaining potatoes. Pour white sauce over all.

3. Bake, covered, for 1 hour. Uncover; sprinkle with cheese. Bake until potatoes are tender, 10-15 minutes longer. If desired, garnish with green onions.

1 CUP: 330 cal., 24g fat (11g sat. fat), 52mg chol., 967mg sod., 18g carb. (4g sugars, 2g fiber), 11g pro.

3 Tbsp. butter
2 Tbsp. all-purpose flour
1 to 1½ tsp. salt
¼ to ½ tsp. pepper
1½ cups 2% milk
5 medium red potatoes, thinly sliced
1 pkg. (1 lb.) hot dogs, halved lengthwise and cut into ½-in. slices
1 medium onion, chopped
⅓ cup shredded cheddar cheese
Chopped green onions, optional

CRANBERRY-KISSED PORK CHOPS

I enjoy coming up with new recipes for my health-conscious family.
I like to serve these pretty chops with cooked noodles or wild rice.
Betty Joan Nichols, Eugene, OR

TAKES: 25 MIN. • **MAKES:** 6 SERVINGS

6 boneless pork loin chops
   (5 oz. each)
¼ tsp. coarsely ground pepper
⅓ cup jellied cranberry sauce
4½ tsp. stone-ground mustard
3 Tbsp. dried cranberries
2 Tbsp. raspberry vinegar

*Save money by making your own
berry vinegar. Recipe on p. 317.*

1. Sprinkle pork chops with pepper. Brown chops on both sides over medium-high heat in a large skillet coated with cooking spray. Combine cranberry sauce and mustard; spoon over chops. Reduce heat; cover and cook for 4-6 minutes or until a thermometer reads 145°.

2. Remove chops and let stand for 5 minutes. Add cranberries and vinegar to skillet, stirring to loosen browned bits from pan. Bring to a boil; cook until liquid is reduced to about ½ cup. Serve with chops.

1 PORK CHOP WITH ABOUT 1 TBSP. SAUCE: 229 cal., 8g fat (3g sat. fat), 68mg chol., 119mg sod., 10g carb. (7g sugars, 1g fiber), 27g pro. **DIABETIC EXCHANGES:** 4 lean meat, 1 starch.

ROAST PORK WITH APPLES & ONIONS

The sweetness of the apples and onions nicely complements the roast pork. With its crisp, golden exterior and melt-in-your-mouth flavor, this pork is my family's favorite weekend dinner.

Lily Julow, Lawrenceville, GA

PREP: 30 MIN. • **BAKE:** 45 MIN. + STANDING • **MAKES:** 8 SERVINGS

1 boneless pork loin roast (2 lbs.)
¼ tsp. salt
¼ tsp. pepper
1 Tbsp. olive oil
3 large Golden Delicious apples, cut into 1-in. wedges
2 large onions, cut into ¾-in. wedges
5 garlic cloves, peeled
1 Tbsp. minced fresh rosemary or 1 tsp. dried rosemary, crushed

1. Preheat oven to 350°. Sprinkle roast with salt and pepper. In a large nonstick skillet, heat oil over medium heat; brown roast on all sides. Transfer to a roasting pan coated with cooking spray. Place apples, onions and garlic around roast; sprinkle with rosemary.

2. Roast until a thermometer inserted in pork reads 145°, 45-55 minutes, turning apples, onion and garlic once. Remove from oven; tent with foil. Let stand for 10 minutes before slicing roast. Serve with apple mixture.

1 SERVING: 210 cal., 7g fat (2g sat. fat), 57mg chol., 109mg sod., 14g carb. (9g sugars, 2g fiber), 23g pro. **DIABETIC EXCHANGES:** 3 lean meat, 1 starch, ½ fat.

BLACKENED PORK CAESAR SALAD

When I cook, the goal is to have enough leftovers for lunch the next day.
This Caesar salad with pork has fantastic flavor even when the meat is chilled.
—*Penny Hedges, Dewdney, BC*

TAKES: 30 MIN. • **MAKES:** 2 SERVINGS

1. For dressing, in a small bowl, mix the first 6 ingredients until blended.

2. Toss pork with blackened seasoning. In a large skillet, heat oil over medium-high heat. Add pork; cook and stir until tender, 5-7 minutes.

3. To serve, place romaine in a large bowl; add dressing and toss to coat. Top with pork and, if desired, croutons and cheese.

2½ CUPS: 458 cal., 31g fat (5g sat. fat), 100mg chol., 464mg sod., 8g carb. (2g sugars, 3g fiber), 36g pro.

2   Tbsp. mayonnaise
1   Tbsp. olive oil
1   Tbsp. lemon juice
1   garlic clove, minced
⅛   tsp. seasoned salt
⅛   tsp. pepper

SALAD
¾   lb. pork tenderloin,
    cut into 1-in. cubes
1   Tbsp. blackened seasoning
1   Tbsp. canola oil
6   cups torn romaine
    Optional: Salad croutons and
    shredded Parmesan cheese

5i

PORK CHOPS WITH APPLES & STUFFING

The heartwarming taste of cinnamon and apples is the perfect
accompaniment to tender pork chops. This dish is always a winner with my family.
Because it calls for only four ingredients, it's a main course I can serve with little preparation.
—*Joan Hamilton, Worcester, MA*

PREP: 15 MIN. • **BAKE:** 45 MIN. • **MAKES:** 6 SERVINGS

1. In a large skillet, brown pork chops in oil over medium-high heat. Meanwhile, prepare stuffing according to package directions. Spread pie filling into a greased 13x9-in. baking dish. Place the pork chops on top; spoon stuffing over chops.

2. Cover and bake at 350° for 35 minutes. Uncover; bake until a thermometer reads 145°, about 10 minutes longer. If desired, sprinkle with parsley.

1 SERVING: 527 cal., 21g fat (9g sat. fat), 102mg chol., 550mg sod., 48g carb. (15g sugars, 3g fiber), 36g pro.

6   boneless pork loin chops
    (6 oz. each)
1   Tbsp. canola oil
1   pkg. (6 oz.) crushed stuffing mix
1   can (21 oz.) apple pie filling
    with cinnamon
    Minced fresh parsley, optional

SICILIAN MEAT SAUCE

People have told me this is better than the gravy their Sicilian grandmothers used to make. But don't tell the older generation that!
—*Emory Doty, Jasper, GA*

PREP: 30 MIN. • **COOK:** 6 HOURS • **MAKES:** 3 QTS.

3 Tbsp. olive oil, divided
3 lbs. bone-in country-style pork ribs
1 medium onion, chopped
3 to 5 garlic cloves, minced
2 cans (28 oz. each) crushed or diced tomatoes, drained
1 can (14½ oz.) Italian diced tomatoes, drained
3 bay leaves
2 Tbsp. chopped fresh parsley or 2 tsp. dried parsley
2 Tbsp. chopped capers, drained
½ tsp. dried basil
½ tsp. dried rosemary, crushed
½ tsp. dried thyme
½ tsp. crushed red pepper flakes
½ tsp. salt
½ tsp. sugar
1 cup beef broth
½ cup dry red wine or additional beef broth
  Hot cooked pasta
  Grated Parmesan cheese, optional

1. In a Dutch oven, heat 2 Tbsp. olive oil over medium-high heat. Brown pork ribs in batches; transfer to a 6-qt. slow cooker.

2. Add remaining oil to Dutch oven; saute onion for 2 minutes. Add garlic; cook 1 minute more. Add next 11 ingredients. Pour in broth and red wine; bring to a light boil. Transfer to slow cooker. Cook, covered, until pork is tender, about 6 hours.

3. Discard bay leaves. Remove meat from slow cooker; shred or pull apart, discarding bones. Return meat to sauce. Serve over pasta; if desired, sprinkle with Parmesan cheese.

¾ CUP: 157 cal., 8g fat (2g sat. fat), 32mg chol., 442mg sod., 11g carb. (7g sugars, 2g fiber), 12g pro.

KEEP PARSLEY UP TO ONE MONTH

Place herb stems in an inch of water (keep leaves out of water). Tie produce bag around the top to trap humidity; chill. Change water and turn bag inside out each time you use the parsley.

BEAN & BACON GRIDDLE BURRITOS

These griddle burritos with bacon and veggies make an awesome hand-held meal.
A jar of salsa works if that's what you've got, but I use fresh pico de gallo when I can.
—*Stacy Mullens, Gresham, OR*

TAKES: 20 MIN. • **MAKES:** 4 SERVINGS

1. In a small bowl, mix beans and ¼ cup salsa until blended. Place tortillas on a griddle; cook over medium heat 1 minute, then turn over. Place bean mixture, cheese and bacon onto centers of tortillas; cook until tortillas begin to crisp, 1-2 minutes longer.

2. Remove from griddle; immediately top with lettuce and remaining salsa. To serve, fold bottom and sides of tortilla over filling.

1 BURRITO: 375 cal., 10g fat (4g sat. fat), 21mg chol., 1133mg sod., 52g carb. (1g sugars, 8g fiber), 18g pro.

1 can (16 oz.) fat-free refried beans
½ cup salsa, divided
4 flour tortillas (8 in.)
½ cup crumbled Cotija cheese or shredded Monterey Jack cheese
3 bacon strips, cooked and coarsely chopped
2 cups shredded lettuce

UPSIDE-DOWN PIZZA BAKE

This super easy but exceptionally delicious recipe is one I've been preparing
and serving to my children and now to my grandchildren for over 30 years!
—Sandy Bastian, Tinley Park, IL

PREP: 20 MIN. • **BAKE:** 25 MIN • **MAKES:** 4 SERVINGS

½ lb. Italian sausage links,
   cut into ¼-in. slices
1 cup spaghetti sauce
½ cup sliced fresh mushrooms
½ cup julienned green pepper
1 cup shredded part-skim
   mozzarella cheese, divided
1 cup biscuit/baking mix
1 large egg
½ cup 2% milk

*Save money by making your own
marinara sauce and biscuit/baking mix.
Recipes on pp. 313 and 304, respectively.*

1. In a large skillet, cook sausage over medium heat until meat is no longer pink; drain.

2. Pour spaghetti sauce into a greased 8-in. square baking dish. Layer with mushrooms, green pepper, sausage and ½ cup cheese.

3. In a small bowl, combine the biscuit mix, egg and milk until blended. Pour over top. Sprinkle with remaining cheese.

4. Bake, uncovered, at 400° for 25-30 minutes or until golden brown.

1 SERVING: 378 cal., 21g fat (8g sat. fat), 96mg chol., 1117mg sod., 28g carb. (8g sugars, 2g fiber), 19g pro.

CLASSIC CAJUN STEW

After 25 years in a place where Cajun cooking is common, we've come to rely on this staple menu item.
If you've never tried red beans and rice before, I assure you that you'll like this recipe.
—*Jackie Turnage, New Iberia, LA*

PREP: 10 MIN. ı STANDING · **COOK:** 2¼ HOURS · **MAKES:** 8 SERVINGS

1   lb. dried kidney beans
8   cups water
1   ham hock
2   bay leaves
1   tsp. onion powder
1   lb. ground pork or ground beef
1   large onion, chopped
1   tsp. salt
½   tsp. pepper
1   garlic clove, minced
    Hot cooked rice
    Chopped fresh parsley, optional

THRIFTY TIP

Beans pack a nutritional one-two punch of protein and fiber that helps you feel fuller longer. They're a green source of protein that can help you economically stretch the meat in a recipe.

1. Sort beans and rinse with cold water. Place beans in a Dutch oven; add enough water to cover by 2 in. Bring to a boil; boil for 2 minutes. Remove from the heat; cover and let stand until beans are softened, 1-4 hours.

2. Drain and rinse beans, discarding liquid. Return to Dutch oven. Add the 8 cups water, ham hock, bay leaves and onion powder. Bring to a boil. Reduce heat; cover and simmer for 1 hour.

3. In a large cast-iron or other heavy skillet, cook the ground pork, onion, salt and pepper over medium heat until meat is no longer pink, breaking pork into crumbles. Add garlic; cook 1 minute longer. Drain. Add to bean mixture. Simmer, uncovered, 1 hour. Discard bay leaves.

4. Remove ham hock; allow to cool. Remove meat from bone; discard bone. Cut meat into bite-sized pieces and return to broth. Heat through. Serve with rice and, if desired, top with chopped fresh parsley.

1 SERVING: 309 cal., 7g fat (3g sat. fat), 35mg chol., 346mg sod., 37g carb. (4g sugars, 9g fiber), 25g pro.

CARNITAS

The house smells fantastic all day when I'm making this slow-cooked recipe.
The tacos have so much flavor, you'd never guess they use just five ingredients.
I love that the meat is ready when you need it at the end of the day.
—*Mary Wood, Maize, KS*

PREP: 15 MIN. • **COOK:** 6 HOURS • **MAKES:** 12 SERVINGS

1 boneless pork shoulder
   butt roast (3 to 4 lbs.)
1 envelope taco seasoning
1 can (10 oz.) diced tomatoes
   and green chiles, undrained
12 flour tortillas (8 in.), warmed
2 cups shredded Colby-
   Monterey Jack cheese
   Sour cream, optional

1. Cut roast in half; place in a 4- or 5-qt. slow cooker. Sprinkle with taco seasoning. Pour tomatoes over top. Cover and cook on low for 6-8 hours or until the meat is tender.

2. Remove meat from slow cooker; shred with 2 forks. Skim fat from cooking juices. Return meat to slow cooker; heat through. Using a slotted spoon, place ½ cup on each tortilla; top with cheese. Serve with sour cream if desired.

1 TACO: 414 cal., 20g fat (8g sat. fat), 84mg chol., 789mg sod., 30g carb. (1g sugars, 0 fiber), 28g pro.

SUNDAY CHOPS & STUFFING

My family likes to make these chops for Sunday dinner.
The recipe lets us spend more time having fun together and less time cooking.
—*Georgiann Franklin, Canfield, OH*

PREP: 30 MIN. • **BAKE:** 25 MIN. • **MAKES:** 6 SERVINGS

1. Preheat oven to 350°. In a large saucepan, combine water, celery, 6 Tbsp. butter and onion. Bring to a boil. Remove from heat; stir in stuffing cubes. Spoon into a greased 13x9-in. baking dish.

2. In a large skillet, heat oil over medium heat. Brown pork chops on both sides. Arrange over stuffing. Sprinkle with salt and pepper. In a small bowl, toss apples with brown sugar and pie spice; place over pork chops. Dot with remaining butter.

3. Bake, uncovered, 25-30 minutes or until a thermometer inserted in pork reads 145°. Let stand 5 minutes before serving.

1 SERVING: 600 cal., 26g fat (12g sat. fat), 122mg chol., 1018mg sod., 56g carb. (19g sugars, 4g fiber), 36g pro

- 2   cups water
- 2   celery ribs, chopped (about 1 cup)
- 7   Tbsp. butter, divided
- ¼   cup dried minced onion
- 6   cups seasoned stuffing cubes
- 1   Tbsp. canola oil
- 6   bone-in pork loin chops (7 oz. each)
- ¼   tsp. salt
- ¼   tsp. pepper
- 2   medium tart apples, sliced
- ¼   cup packed brown sugar
- ⅛   tsp. pumpkin pie spice

MY TWO CENTS

"I didn't use the baking dish. After browning the chops, I sweated the onion and celery in the same pan. I made the stuffing in the pan also, then placed it all in the oven. I try to eliminate extra cleanup!"

—GEORGEREID, TASTEOFHOME.COM

5i
SAUSAGE & SPINACH CALZONES

These comforting calzones are perfect for quick meals—or even midnight snacks.
My nurse co-workers always ask me to make them when it's my turn to bring in lunch.
—*Kourtney Williams, Mechanicsville, VA*

TAKES: 30 MIN. • **MAKES:** 4 SERVINGS

½ lb. bulk Italian sausage
3 cups fresh baby spinach
1 tube (13.8 oz.) refrigerated pizza crust
¾ cup shredded part-skim mozzarella cheese
½ cup part-skim ricotta cheese
¼ tsp. pepper
Pizza sauce, optional

*Save money by making your own pizza dough. Recipe on p. 316.

1. Preheat oven to 400°. In a large skillet, cook and crumble the sausage over medium heat until no longer pink, 4-6 minutes; drain. Add spinach; cook and stir until wilted. Remove from heat.

2. On a lightly floured surface, unroll and pat dough into a 15x11-in. rectangle. Cut into 4 rectangles. Sprinkle mozzarella cheese on half of each rectangle to within 1 in. of edges.

3. Stir ricotta cheese and pepper into sausage mixture; spoon over mozzarella cheese. Fold dough over filling; press edges with a fork to seal. Place on a greased baking sheet.

4. Bake until light golden brown, 10-15 minutes. If desired, serve with pizza sauce.

FREEZE OPTION: Freeze cooled calzones in an airtight freezer container. To use, microwave calzone on high until heated through.

1 CALZONE: 489 cal., 22g fat (9g sat. fat), 54mg chol., 1242mg sod., 51g carb. (7g sugars, 2g fiber), 23g pro.

LORA'S RED BEANS & RICE

My dear mother-in-law passed this simple recipe to me. With meats, beans and savory veggies that simmer all day, it's tasty, easy and economical too!
—*Carol Simms, Madison, MS*

PREP: 15 MIN. + SOAKING • **COOK:** 8 HOURS • **MAKES:** 10 SERVINGS

1. Place beans in a large bowl; add cool water to cover. Soak overnight.

2. Drain beans, discarding water; rinse with cool water. Place beans in a greased 6-qt. slow cooker. Stir in ham, sausage, vegetables, pepper sauce, garlic and salt. Add water to cover by 1 in.

3. Cook, covered, on low 8-9 hours or until beans are tender. Serve with rice.

1 CUP BEAN MIXTURE: 249 cal., 5g fat (1g sat. fat), 43mg chol., 906mg sod., 31g carb. (2g sugars, 7g fiber), 23g pro.

1   lb. dried kidney beans (about 2½ cups)
2   cups cubed fully cooked ham (about 1 lb.)
1   pkg. (12 oz.) fully cooked andouille chicken sausage links or flavor of choice, sliced
1   medium green pepper, chopped
1   medium onion, chopped
2   celery ribs, chopped
1   Tbsp. hot pepper sauce
2   garlic cloves, minced
1½ tsp. salt
    Hot cooked rice

REVIVE LIMP CELERY

It's easy to give limp celery a second chance to season entrees, soups and stews. Cut the ends from the stalks and place stalks in a glass of cold water in the refrigerator for several hours or overnight. You will be surprised how the celery becomes refreshed.

POLISH KRAUT & APPLES

My family loves this hearty meal on cold winter nights. The tender apples, kraut and smoked sausage give it a heartwarming old-world flavor. I like making it because the prep time is very short.
—*Caren Markee, Cary, IL*

PREP: 10 MIN. • **COOK:** 4 HOURS • **MAKES:** 4 SERVINGS

1 can (14 oz.) sauerkraut, rinsed and well drained
1 lb. smoked Polish sausage or kielbasa, cut up
3 medium tart apples, peeled and cut into eighths
½ cup packed brown sugar
½ tsp. caraway seeds, optional
⅛ tsp. pepper
¾ cup apple juice

1. Place half the sauerkraut in an ungreased 3-qt. slow cooker. Top with sausage, apples, brown sugar, caraway seeds if desired, and pepper. Top with remaining sauerkraut. Pour apple juice over all.

2. Cover and cook on low until apples are tender, 4-5 hours.

1 CUP: 546 cal., 31g fat (12g sat. fat), 81mg chol., 1630mg sod., 52g carb. (43g sugars, 4g fiber), 15g pro.

SLOW-COOKER TURKEY BREAST

Try this easy-to-fix, wonderfully flavored, tender slow-cooker entree when you're craving turkey.
—*Maria Juco, Milwaukee, WI*

PREP: 10 MIN. • **COOK:** 5 HOURS • **MAKES:** 14 SERVINGS

1 bone-in turkey breast
   (6 to 7 lbs.), skin removed
1 Tbsp. olive oil
1 tsp. dried minced garlic
1 tsp. seasoned salt
1 tsp. paprika
1 tsp. Italian seasoning
1 tsp. pepper
½ cup water

Brush turkey with oil. Combine the garlic, seasoned salt, paprika, Italian seasoning and pepper; rub over turkey. Transfer to a 6-qt. slow cooker; add water. Cover and cook on low for 5-6 hours or until tender.

4 OZ. COOKED TURKEY: 173 cal., 2g fat (0 sat. fat), 100mg chol., 171mg sod., 0 carb. (0 sugars, 0 fiber), 36g pro. **DIABETIC EXCHANGES:** 4 lean meat.

LEMON-GARLIC TURKEY BREAST: Combine ¼ cup minced fresh parsley, 8 minced garlic cloves, 4 tsp. grated lemon zest, 2 tsp. salt-free lemon-pepper seasoning and 1½ tsp. salt; rub over turkey breast. Add water and cook as directed.

DIY ITALIAN SEASONING

If you don't have Italian seasoning, you can make your own with equal amounts of basil, thyme, rosemary and oregano. You can also add in parsley flakes, marjoram, sage, savory or garlic powder.

CHICKEN NOODLE CASSEROLE

Everyone who tries this comforting cheesy chicken casserole asks for the recipe.
It's so simple to make that sometimes I feel as if I'm cheating!
—*Kay Pederson, Yellville, AR*

PREP: 15 MIN. • **BAKE:** 40 MIN. • **MAKES:** 6 SERVINGS

1. In a large bowl, combine the soup, mayonnaise and lemon juice. Stir in chicken, onion, peppers, ½ cup Monterey Jack cheese and ½ cup cheddar cheese. Add noodles and toss to coat.

2. Transfer to a greased 2-qt. baking dish. Bake, uncovered, at 350° for 30-35 minutes. Sprinkle with the remaining cheeses. Bake until cheese is melted, about 10 minutes longer.

FREEZE OPTION: Sprinkle remaining cheeses over unbaked casserole. Cover and freeze. To use, partially thaw in refrigerator overnight. Remove from refrigerator 30 minutes before baking. Preheat oven to 350°. Bake casserole as directed, increasing time as necessary to heat through and for a thermometer inserted in center to read 165°.

1 CUP: 632 cal., 35g fat (12g sat. fat), 130mg chol., 751mg sod., 47g carb. (3g sugars, 3g fiber), 32g pro.

- 1   can (10¾ oz.) condensed cream of chicken soup, undiluted
- ½   cup mayonnaise
- 2   Tbsp. lemon juice
- 2   cups cubed cooked chicken
- 1   small onion, chopped
- ¼   cup chopped green pepper
- ¼   cup chopped sweet red pepper
- 1   cup shredded Monterey Jack cheese, divided
- 1   cup shredded sharp cheddar cheese, divided
- 12 oz. egg noodles, cooked and drained

THRIFTY SWAP

Green bell peppers are actually unripened versions of the sweeter-tasting colored peppers. They're less expensive than sweet peppers because they're faster to market. To save time and money, use whatever color pepper you like instead of mixing the different colors.

CAROLINA-STYLE VINEGAR BBQ CHICKEN

I live in Georgia but I appreciate the tangy, sweet and slightly spicy taste of Carolina vinegar chicken. I make my version in the slow cooker. With the tempting aroma filling the house, your family is sure to be at the dinner table on time!
—*Ramona Parris, Canton, GA*

PREP: 10 MIN. • **COOK:** 4 HOURS • **MAKES:** 6 SERVINGS

1. In a small bowl, mix the first 6 ingredients. Place chicken in a 3-qt. slow cooker; add vinegar mixture. Cook, covered, on low 4-5 hours or until chicken is tender.

2. Remove chicken; cool slightly. Reserve 1 cup cooking juices; discard remaining juices. Shred chicken with 2 forks. Return meat and reserved cooking juices to slow cooker; heat through. If desired, serve chicken mixture on buns.

NOTE: Look for chicken base near the broth and bouillon.

½ CUP: 134 cal., 3g fat (1g sat. fat), 63mg chol., 228mg sod., 3g carb. (3g sugars, 0 fiber), 23g pro. **DIABETIC EXCHANGES:** 3 lean meat.

- 2 cups water
- 1 cup white vinegar
- ¼ cup sugar
- 1 Tbsp. reduced-sodium chicken base
- 1 tsp. crushed red pepper flakes
- ¾ tsp. salt
- 1½ lbs. boneless skinless chicken breasts
- 6 whole wheat hamburger buns, split, optional

TIMESAVING TECHNIQUE

Make fast work of shredding chicken with your stand mixer's paddle attachment.

RAMEN-VEGGIE CHICKEN SALAD

Like a salad with plenty of crunch? Then this refreshing recipe is sure to please. Toasted noodles, almonds and sesame seeds provide the crunchy topping. The chicken makes it a main dish.
—*Linda Gearhart, Greensboro, NC*

PREP: 30 MIN. • **GRILL:** 10 MIN. • **MAKES:** 2 SERVINGS

¼ cup sugar
¼ cup canola oil
2 Tbsp. cider vinegar
1 Tbsp. reduced-sodium soy sauce
1 pkg. (3 oz.) ramen noodles
1 Tbsp. butter
⅓ cup sliced almonds
1 Tbsp. sesame seeds
1 boneless skinless
  chicken breast half (6 oz.)
4 cups shredded Chinese
  or napa cabbage
½ large sweet red pepper,
  thinly sliced
3 green onions, thinly sliced
1 medium carrot, julienned

1. In a small saucepan, combine the sugar, oil, vinegar and soy sauce. Bring to a boil, cook and stir until sugar is dissolved, about 1 minute; set aside to cool.

2. Meanwhile, break noodles into small pieces (save seasoning packet for another use). In a small skillet, melt butter over medium heat. Add the noodles, almonds and sesame seeds; cook and stir until lightly toasted, 1-2 minutes.

3. Grill chicken, covered, over medium heat until a thermometer reads 165°, 4-6 minutes on each side.

4. Meanwhile, arrange the cabbage, red pepper, onions and carrot on 2 serving plates. Slice chicken; place on salad. Top with noodle mixture; drizzle with dressing.

1 SERVING: 865 cal., 53g fat (11g sat. fat), 62mg chol., 574mg sod., 68g carb. (32g sugars, 7g fiber), 29g pro.

GARLIC-GINGER TURKEY TENDERLOINS

This good-for-you entree can be on your dinner plates quicker than Chinese takeout—and
for a lot less money! Ginger and brown sugar flavor the sauce that spices up the turkey as it bakes.
—Taste of Home *Test Kitchen*

TAKES: 30 MIN. • **MAKES:** 4 SERVINGS

1. Preheat oven to 375°. In a small saucepan, mix 2 Tbsp. brown sugar, 2 Tbsp. soy sauce, ginger, garlic and pepper.

2. Place turkey in a 13x9-in. baking dish coated with cooking spray; drizzle with half the soy sauce mixture. Bake, uncovered, until a thermometer reads 165°, 25-30 minutes.

3. Meanwhile, add cornstarch and the remaining brown sugar and soy sauce to the remaining mixture in saucepan; stir until smooth. Stir in broth. Bring to a boil; cook and stir until thickened, 1-2 minutes. Cut turkey into slices; serve with sauce.

4 OZ. COOKED TURKEY WITH 2 TBSP. SAUCE : 212 cal., 2g fat (1g sat. fat), 69mg chol., 639mg sod., 14g carb. (10g sugars, 0 fiber), 35g pro. **DIABETIC EXCHANGES:** 4 lean meat, 1 starch.

3 Tbsp. brown sugar, divided
2 Tbsp. plus 2 tsp. reduced-sodium
    soy sauce, divided
2 Tbsp. minced fresh gingerroot
6 garlic cloves, minced
½ tsp. pepper
1 pkg. (20 oz.) turkey breast
    tenderloins
1 Tbsp. cornstarch
1 cup reduced-sodium
    chicken broth

MY TWO CENTS
*"Wonderful! We used
chicken breasts
instead of turkey and
powdered ginger
instead of fresh
because they
were what we
had on hand."*

—ALLISONO, TASTEOFHOME.COM

SAUSAGE-STUFFED BUTTERNUT SQUASH

Load butternut squash shells with an Italian turkey sausage and squash
mixture for a quick and easy meal. Even better, it's surprisingly low in calories.
Katia Slinger, West Jordan, UT

TAKES: 30 MIN. • **MAKES:** 4 SERVINGS

1 medium butternut squash
 (about 3 lbs.)
1 lb. Italian turkey sausage links,
 casings removed
1 medium onion, finely chopped
4 garlic cloves, minced
½ cup shredded
 Italian cheese blend
 Crushed red pepper flakes,
 optional

1. Preheat broiler. Cut squash lengthwise in half; discard seeds. Place squash in a large microwave-safe dish, cut side down; add ½ in. water. Microwave, covered, on high until soft, 20-25 minutes. Cool slightly.

2. Meanwhile, in a large nonstick skillet, cook and crumble sausage with onion over medium-high heat until meat is no longer pink, 5-7 minutes. Add garlic; cook and stir 1 minute.

3. Leaving ½-in.-thick shells, scoop flesh from squash and stir it into sausage mixture. Place squash shells on a baking sheet; fill with sausage mixture. Sprinkle with cheese.

4. Broil 4-5 in. from heat until cheese is melted, 1-2 minutes. If desired, sprinkle with pepper flakes. To serve, cut each half into 2 portions.

1 SERVING: 325 cal., 10g fat (4g sat. fat), 52mg chol., 587mg sod., 44g carb. (10g sugars, 12g fiber), 19g pro. **DIABETIC EXCHANGES:** 3 starch, 3 lean meat.

FETA CHICKEN BURGERS

My friends always request these tasty chicken burgers on the grill.
I sometimes add olives to punch up the flavor! Try them with the mayo topping.
—*Angela Robinson, Findlay, OH*

TAKES: 30 MIN. • **MAKES:** 6 SERVINGS

¼ cup finely chopped cucumber
¼ cup reduced-fat mayonnaise

BURGERS
½ cup chopped roasted
   sweet red pepper
1 tsp. garlic powder
½ tsp. Greek seasoning
¼ tsp. pepper
1½ lbs. lean ground chicken
1 cup crumbled feta cheese
6 whole wheat hamburger buns,
   split and toasted
   Optional: Lettuce leaves and
   tomato slices

1. Preheat broiler. Mix cucumber and mayonnaise. For burgers, mix red pepper and seasonings. Add chicken and cheese; mix lightly but thoroughly (mixture will be sticky). Shape into six ½-in.-thick patties.

2. Broil burgers 4 in. from heat until a thermometer reads 165°, 3-4 minutes per side. Serve on buns with cucumber sauce. If desired, top with lettuce and tomato.

FREEZE OPTION: Place uncooked patties on a waxed paper-lined baking sheet; cover and freeze until firm. Remove from pan and transfer to an airtight freezer container; return to freezer. To use, broil frozen patties as directed, increasing time as necessary.

1 BURGER WITH 1 TBSP. SAUCE: 356 cal., 14g fat (5g sat. fat), 95mg chol., 703mg sod., 25g carb. (5g sugars, 4g fiber), 31g pro. **DIABETIC EXCHANGES:** 5 lean meat, 2 starch, ½ fat.

GRILLED HUMMUS TURKEY SANDWICH

I created this toasted sandwich last summer using homemade
hummus and veggies from our garden. We really can't get enough!
—*Gunjan Gilbert, Franklin, ME*

TAKES: 15 MIN. • **MAKES:** 2 SERVINGS

1. Spread hummus on 2 bread slices; top with turkey, tomato, cheese and remaining bread. Spread outsides of sandwiches with butter.

2. In a large skillet, toast sandwiches over medium heat until golden brown and cheese is melted, 2-3 minutes per side.

1 SANDWICH: 458 cal., 23g fat (10g sat. fat), 63mg chol., 1183mg sod., 36g carb. (3g sugars, 7g fiber), 28g pro.

½ cup hummus
4 slices whole wheat bread
4 oz. thinly sliced deli turkey
4 slices tomato
2 slices pepper jack cheese
4 tsp. butter, softened

*Save money by making your own hummus. Recipe on p. 311.

TURKEY LO MEIN

I substituted turkey for pork in this classic Chinese recipe.
It was a hit at our church potluck, and my husband and two children love it too.
—*Leigh Lundy, York, NE*

TAKES: 30 MIN. • **MAKES:** 6 SERVINGS

1. In a large skillet, cook and crumble turkey with carrots, onion and garlic powder over medium-high heat until meat is until no longer pink, 5-7 minutes.

2. Break up noodles and add to skillet; stir in contents of seasoning packets and water. Bring to a boil. Reduce heat; simmer, covered, 3-5 minutes. Add remaining ingredients; cook and stir until cabbage is crisp-tender, 1-3 minutes.

1⅓ CUPS: 294 cal., 11g fat (4g sat. fat), 52mg chol., 1024mg sod., 28g carb. (3g sugars, 4g fiber), 21g pro.

1   lb. lean ground turkey
2   medium carrots, thinly sliced
1   medium onion, chopped
½   tsp. garlic powder
2   pkg. (3 oz. each) chicken
     ramen noodles
1½ cups water
6   cups shredded cabbage
1   cup frozen peas, thawed
¼   cup reduced-sodium soy sauce

MY TWO CENTS
"So quick and delicious. I buy the pre-shredded carrots and a bag of coleslaw mix from the produce section. What could be easier? The turkey browns nicely without any oil."

BOATIEGIRL, TASTEOFHOME.COM

(5i)

CONTEST-WINNING BROCCOLI CHICKEN CASSEROLE

This delicious twist on chicken divan came from an old boss, who gave
the recipe to me when I got married. It's quick, satisfying comfort food.
—*Jennifer Schlachter, Big Rock, IL*

PREP: 15 MIN. • **BAKE:** 30 MIN. • **MAKES:** 6 SERVINGS

---

1 pkg. (6 oz.) chicken stuffing mix
2 cups cubed cooked chicken
1 cup frozen broccoli florets,
   thawed
1 can (10¾ oz.) condensed
   broccoli cheese soup, undiluted
1 cup shredded cheddar cheese

1. Preheat oven to 350°. Prepare stuffing mix according to package directions, using only 1½ cups water.

2. In large bowl, combine chicken, broccoli and soup; transfer to a greased 11x7-in. baking dish. Top with stuffing; sprinkle with cheese. Bake, covered, 20 minutes. Uncover; bake until heated through, 10-15 minutes longer.

FREEZE OPTION: Transfer individual portions of cooled casserole to freezer containers; freeze. To use, partially thaw in refrigerator overnight. Transfer to a microwave-safe dish and microwave, covered, on high until a thermometer inserted in center reads 165°, stirring occasionally; add a little broth if necessary.

1⅓ CUPS: 315 cal., 13g fat (6g sat. fat), 66mg chol., 1025mg sod., 25g carb. (4g sugars, 2g fiber), 23g pro.

MY TWO CENTS
*"Wow, was that good!
I did double the
chicken and soup but,
oh my goodness,
was this awesome.
And so simple!"*
—ELIZABETH7593, TASTEOFHOME.COM

CHICKEN STEW WITH GNOCCHI

My chicken stew fills the house with a delectable scent as it gently bubbles in the slow cooker. One whiff and my family heads to the kitchen to see if it's ready.
—Marge Drake, Juniata, NE

PREP: 25 MIN. • **COOK:** 6½ HOURS • **MAKES:** 8 SERVINGS (3 QT.)

1. Place the parsnips, carrots, celery, sweet potato and onions in a 5-qt. slow cooker. Top with chicken; sprinkle with the sage, salt and pepper. Add broth and 1 cup water. Cover and cook on low for 6-8 hours or until chicken is tender.

2. Remove chicken; when cool enough to handle, remove meat from bones and discard bones. Cut meat into bite-sized pieces and return to the slow cooker.

3. Mix cornstarch and cold water until smooth; stir into stew. Add gnocchi. Cover and cook on high for 30 minutes or until thickened. If desired, season with hot pepper sauce and sprinkle with sliced green onions.

1½ CUPS: 405 cal., 11g fat (3g sat. fat), 92mg chol., 922mg sod., 46g carb. (10g sugars, 5g fiber), 29g pro.

STOVETOP CHICKEN STEW WITH GNOCCHI: Cover and simmer the chicken, broth, water and seasonings in a Dutch oven for 1 hour. Add the vegetables; cover and simmer 30 minutes longer. Cut chicken and add cornstarch mixture as directed. Add gnocchi. Bring to a boil; cook and stir for 2-3 minutes or until thickened and gnocchi float to the top. Season as directed.

3 medium parsnips, peeled and cut into ½-in. pieces
2 large carrots, cut into ½-in. slices
2 celery ribs, chopped
1 large sweet potato, peeled and cut into 1-in. cubes
4 green onions, chopped
3 lbs. bone-in chicken thighs, skin removed
½ tsp. dried sage leaves
¼ tsp. salt
¼ tsp. pepper
4 cups chicken broth
1 cup water
3 Tbsp. cornstarch
¼ cup cold water
1 pkg. (16 oz.) potato gnocchi
Optional: Hot pepper sauce and thinly sliced green onions

SIMPLE SUBSTITUTION

Parsnips are a bit like herbaceous white carrots. If you can't find parsnips for this recipe, substitute 3 sliced carrots or 2 chopped turnips.

SWISS TURKEY STROMBOLI

Similar to a calzone, stromboli is a type of turnover. Pizza dough is stuffed with various cheeses, meats and veggies and then baked. Use this simple recipe to experiment with your favorite flavor combinations.
Taste of Home *Test Kitchen*

PREP: 25 MIN. • **BAKE:** 15 MIN. + STANDING • **MAKES:** 4 SERVINGS

1. In a large nonstick skillet, saute mushrooms and onion in oil until tender. Stir in mustard; set aside.

2. On a floured surface, roll dough into a 15x10-in. rectangle. Layer the cheese, mushroom mixture and turkey lengthwise over half the dough to within ½ in. of edges. Fold dough over filling; pinch seams to seal and tuck ends under. Transfer to a baking sheet coated with cooking spray.

3. Combine egg white and water; brush over dough. Cut slits in top. Bake at 400° for 12-15 minutes or until golden brown. Let stand for 10 minutes before cutting.

1 PIECE: 385 cal., 12g fat (2g sat. fat), 23mg chol., 804mg sod., 50g carb. (5g sugars, 5g fiber), 23g pro.

3   cups sliced fresh mushrooms
1   medium onion, chopped
1   Tbsp. canola oil
2   Tbsp. spicy brown mustard
1   lb. pizza dough
3   slices reduced-fat Swiss cheese
6   oz. sliced deli turkey
1   large egg white
1   tsp. water

Save money by making your own pizza dough. Recipe on p. 316.

BBQ CHICKEN & SMOKED SAUSAGE

My party-ready barbecue recipe works like a dream for weeknights too.
With just a few minutes of prep time, you still get that low-and-slow flavor everybody
craves (thanks, slow cooker!). Throw in minced jalapenos for extra oomph.
—*Kimberly Young, Mesquite, TX*

PREP: 30 MIN. • **COOK:** 4 HOURS • **MAKES:** 8 SERVINGS

1   medium onion, chopped
1   large sweet red pepper,
    cut into 1-in. pieces
4   bone-in chicken thighs,
    skin removed
4   chicken drumsticks,
    skin removed
1   pkg. (12 oz.) smoked sausage
    links, cut into 1-in. pieces
1   cup barbecue sauce
    Sliced seeded jalapeno pepper,
    optional

1. Place first 5 ingredients in a 4- or 5-qt. slow cooker; top with barbecue sauce. Cook, covered, on low 4-5 hours or until chicken is tender and a thermometer inserted in chicken reads at least 170°-175°.

2. Remove chicken, sausage and vegetables from slow cooker; keep warm. Transfer cooking juices to a saucepan; bring to a boil. Reduce heat; simmer, uncovered, until thickened, 15-20 minutes, stirring occasionally.

3. Serve chicken, sausage and vegetables with sauce. If desired, top with sliced jalapeno.

1 SERVING: 331 cal., 18g fat (6g sat. fat), 91mg chol., 840mg sod., 17g carb. (13g sugars, 1g fiber), 24g pro.

SLOW-COOKED TURKEY SLOPPY JOES

This tangy sandwich filling is so easy to prepare in the slow cooker, and it goes over well at gatherings large and small. I frequently take it to potlucks, and I'm always asked for my secret ingredient.
—*Marylou LaRue, Freeland, MI*

PREP: 15 MIN. • **COOK:** 4 HOURS • **MAKES:** 8 SERVINGS

1. In a large skillet coated with cooking spray, cook turkey, onion, celery and green pepper over medium heat until meat is no longer pink, breaking it into crumbles; drain. Stir in soup, ketchup, mustard, brown sugar and pepper.

2. Transfer to a 3-qt. slow cooker. Cover and cook on low to allow flavors to blend, about 4 hours. Serve on buns.

1 SANDWICH: 264 cal., 7g fat (2g sat. fat), 39mg chol., 614mg sod., 34g carb. (13g sugars, 2g fiber), 16g pro. **DIABETIC EXCHANGES:** 2 starch, 1½ lean meat.

- 1 lb. lean ground turkey
- 1 small onion, chopped
- ½ cup chopped celery
- ¼ cup chopped green pepper
- 1 can (10¾ oz.) reduced-sodium condensed tomato soup, undiluted
- ½ cup ketchup
- 2 Tbsp. prepared mustard
- 1 Tbsp. brown sugar
- ¼ tsp. pepper
- 8 hamburger buns, split

TIMESAVING TIP

The slow cooker allows for easy hands-off cooking and a meal that's ready to eat several hours after you prepare it. But slow-cooking isn't necessary. If you prefer, just simmer the ingredients on the stovetop to allow flavors to blend, stirring occasionally, until the veggies are tender. It'll take about 15 minutes.

PAN-ROASTED CHICKEN & VEGETABLES

This one-dish meal tastes as if it took hours of hands-on time, but the simple ingredients can be prepped in minutes. The rosemary gives it a rich flavor, and the meat juices cook the veggies to perfection. So easy!
—Sherri Melotik, Oak Creek, WI

PREP: 15 MIN. • **BAKE:** 45 MIN. • **MAKES:** 6 SERVINGS

1. Preheat oven to 425°. In a large bowl, combine potatoes, onion, oil, garlic, ¾ tsp. salt, 2 tsp. fresh rosemary or ½ tsp. dried rosemary, and ½ tsp. pepper; toss to coat. Transfer to a 15x10x1-in. baking pan coated with cooking spray.

2. In a small bowl, mix paprika and the remaining salt, rosemary and pepper. Sprinkle chicken with paprika mixture; arrange over vegetables. Roast until a thermometer inserted in chicken reads 170°-175° and vegetables are just tender, 35-40 minutes.

3. Remove chicken to a serving platter; keep warm. Top vegetables with spinach. Roast until vegetables are tender and spinach is wilted, 8-10 minutes longer. Stir vegetables to combine; serve with chicken. If desired, serve with additional fresh rosemary and lemon wedges.

1 CHICKEN THIGH WITH 1 CUP VEGETABLES: 357 cal., 14g fat (3g sat. fat), 87mg chol., 597mg sod., 28g carb. (3g sugars, 4g fiber), 28g pro. **DIABETIC EXCHANGES:** 4 lean meat, 1½ starch, 1 vegetable, 1 fat.

2   lbs. red potatoes
    (about 6 medium),
    cut into ¾-in. pieces
1   large onion, coarsely chopped
2   Tbsp. olive oil
3   garlic cloves, minced
1¼ tsp. salt, divided
1   Tbsp. minced fresh rosemary
    or 1 tsp. dried rosemary,
    crushed, divided
¾   tsp. pepper, divided
½   tsp. paprika
6   bone-in chicken thighs
    (about 2¼ lbs.), skin removed
6   cups fresh baby spinach
    (about 6 oz.)
    Lemon wedges, optional

CHICKEN CORDON BLEU SKILLET

Here's a good and hearty supper. If I have fresh mushrooms on hand, I slice them and toss them in the skillet. You could add cooked veggies like broccoli or cauliflower too.
—Sandy Harz, Spring Lake, MI

TAKES: 25 MIN • MAKES: 4 SERVINGS

8   oz. uncooked medium
    egg noodles (about 5 cups)
1   lb. boneless skinless
    chicken breasts,
    cut in 1-in. pieces
½   tsp. pepper
1   Tbsp. butter
1   can (10¾ oz.) condensed
    cream of chicken soup, undiluted
½   cup shredded Swiss cheese
½   cup cubed fully cooked ham
¼   cup water
    Minced fresh parsley

1. Cook noodles according to package directions; drain.

2. Meanwhile, sprinkle chicken with pepper. In a large cast-iron or other heavy skillet, heat butter over medium-high heat; saute chicken just until browned, 3-5 minutes. Stir in soup, cheese, ham and water; cook, covered, over medium heat until cheese is melted and chicken is no longer pink, 6-8 minutes, stirring occasionally. Stir in noodles. Sprinkle with parsley.

1½ CUPS: 516 cal., 18g fat (8g sat. fat), 147mg chol., 878mg sod., 47g carb. (2g sugars, 3g fiber), 40g pro.

MY TWO CENTS
"This recipe was good. I added a bag of frozen broccoli and it was a whole meal!"
—COLLEENAG, TASTEOFHOME.COM

HEALTHIER-THAN-EGG ROLLS

*Frying anything at home can be a little intimidating for me, but I love egg rolls.
With this recipe, I've figured out a way to get the best part without the mess.
This can be used to stuff egg roll wrappers, but we love it on its own too.*
—*Sue Mitchell, Kerrville, TX*

TAKES: 25 MIN. • **MAKES:** 4 SERVINGS

1. In a large cast-iron or other heavy skillet, cook and crumble chicken with mushrooms, onion, garlic and ginger over medium-high heat until no longer pink, 6-8 minutes; drain. Stir in soy sauce.

2. Add coleslaw mix; cook and stir until wilted, 3-4 minutes. Stir in sesame oil. Serve with rice and sweet-and-sour sauce. If desired, top with wonton strips.

1¼ CUPS CHICKEN MIXTURE WITH ¾ CUP RICE: 451 cal., 11g fat (3g sat. fat), 81mg chol., 591mg sod., 58g carb. (13g sugars, 6g fiber), 30g pro.

1   lb. lean ground chicken
1½ cups sliced fresh mushrooms
1   medium onion, chopped
2   garlic cloves, minced
1   tsp. minced fresh gingerroot
2   Tbsp. reduced-sodium soy sauce
1   pkg. (14 oz.) coleslaw mix
1   Tbsp. sesame oil
3   cups hot cooked brown rice
½   cup sweet-and-sour sauce
     Wonton strips, optional

SAVE SOME CASH

Sesame oil adds a nutty flavor and complexity to this dish, but it is expensive. If you don't want to splurge on a bottle, you can get a nutty flavor by sprinkling the dish with chopped roasted peanuts or toasted sesame seeds.

SLOW-COOKER TURKEY PESTO LASAGNA

My cheesy, noodle-y lasagna makes any slow-cooker skeptic a believer.
It's easy to prep while my kids nap, and dinner's ready when their dad walks in the door at night.
We bring more pesto and marinara to the table for our resident sauce lovers.
—*Blair Lonergan, Rochelle, VA*

PREP: 25 MIN. • **COOK:** 3 HOURS + STANDING • **MAKES:** 8 SERVINGS

1   lb. ground turkey
1   small onion, chopped
2   tsp. Italian seasoning
½   tsp. salt
2   cups shredded part-skim
    mozzarella cheese, divided
1   container (15 oz.) whole-milk
    ricotta cheese
¼   cup prepared pesto
1   jar (24 oz.) marinara sauce
9   no-cook lasagna noodles
    Grated Parmesan cheese

**Save money by making your own
pesto and marinara sauce. Recipes
on pp. 309 and 313, respectively.*

1. Cut three 25x3-in. strips of heavy-duty foil; crisscross so they resemble spokes of a wheel. Place strips on bottom and up sides of a greased 5-qt. slow cooker. Coat strips with cooking spray.

2. In a large skillet, cook turkey and onion over medium heat 6-8 minutes or until turkey is no longer pink, breaking turkey into crumbles; drain. Stir in Italian seasoning and salt.

3. In a small bowl, mix 1 cup mozzarella cheese, ricotta cheese and pesto. In prepared slow cooker, layer a third each of the following: marinara sauce, noodles (breaking noodles if necessary to fit), turkey mixture and cheese mixture. Repeat layers twice. Sprinkle with remaining mozzarella cheese.

4. Cook, covered, on low until noodles are tender, 3-4 hours. Turn off slow cooker; remove insert. Let stand, uncovered, 30 minutes before serving. Using foil strips, remove lasagna to a platter. Serve with Parmesan cheese.

1 PIECE: 397 cal., 19g fat (8g sat. fat), 79mg chol., 883mg sod., 28g carb. (9g sugars, 3g fiber), 28g pro.

CHICKEN & DUMPLINGS

Perfect for fall nights, my simple version of comforting chicken and
dumplings is speedy, low in fat and a delicious one-dish meal.
—*Nancy Tuck, Elk Falls, KS*

TAKES: 30 MIN. • **MAKES:** 6 SERVINGS

---

3 celery ribs, chopped
2 medium carrots, sliced
3 cans (14½ oz. each)
    reduced-sodium chicken broth
3 cups cubed cooked
    chicken breast
½ tsp. poultry seasoning
⅛ tsp. pepper
1⅔ cups reduced-fat
    biscuit/baking mix
⅔ cup fat-free milk

*Save money by making your own
biscuit/baking mix. Recipe on p. 304.*

1. In a Dutch oven coated with cooking spray, cook and stir celery and carrots over medium heat until tender, about 5 minutes. Stir in broth, chicken and seasonings. Bring to a boil; reduce heat to a gentle simmer.

2. For dumplings, mix biscuit mix and milk until a soft dough forms. Drop by tablespoonfuls on top of the simmering liquid. Reduce heat to low; cover and cook until a toothpick inserted in dumplings comes out clean (do not lift cover during the first 10 minutes), 10-15 minutes.

1 CUP: 260 cal., 4g fat (1g sat. fat), 54mg chol., 964mg sod., 28g carb. (6g sugars, 2g fiber), 27g pro.

ROAST SPICED CHICKEN

My mother's index card recipe is worn and food stains obscure the words—that's how much I've cooked this dish. Spiced chicken has been in our family more than 50 years.
—*Cindy Kanwar, Blacklick, OH*

PREP: 20 MIN. • **BAKE:** 1½ HOURS + STANDING • **MAKES:** 12 SERVINGS

1. Preheat oven to 425°. In a small bowl, mix the first 5 ingredients. In a small saucepan, melt butter; stir in lemon juice, mustard, paprika and garlic salt. Keep warm.

2. Sprinkle half the thyme mixture inside chicken; if desired, place quartered lemon inside chicken. Place chicken on a rack in a shallow roasting pan, breast side up. Tuck wings under chicken; tie drumsticks together.

3. Brush outside of chicken with ½ cup butter mixture; sprinkle with remaining thyme mixture. Roast 1 hour, basting every 15 minutes with remaining butter mixture. (Cover loosely with foil if chicken browns too quickly.)

4. Roast until a thermometer inserted in thickest part of thigh reads 170°-175°, 30-60 minutes longer. Remove chicken from oven; tent with foil. Let stand 15 minutes before carving.

1 SERVING: 390 cal., 27g fat (11g sat. fat), 132mg chol., 918mg sod., 2g carb. (0 sugars, 0 fiber), 33g pro.

- 3 tsp. dried thyme
- 2 tsp. salt
- 2 tsp. seasoned salt
- 2 tsp. pepper
- ½ tsp. garlic powder
- ⅔ cup butter, cubed
- ⅓ cup lemon juice
- 2 Tbsp. Dijon mustard
- 1½ tsp. paprika
- ½ tsp. garlic salt
- 1 roasting chicken (6 to 7 lbs.)
- 1 lemon, quartered, optional

THRIFTY TIP

Make your own homemade broth from the chicken carcass. Recipe on p. 305.

MINI TURKEY MEAT LOAVES

I love this quick and easy dish. The turkey loaves are tender, hearty and loaded with flavor.
—*Janice Christofferson, Eagle River, WI*

PREP: 25 MIN. • **BAKE:** 25 MIN. • **MAKES:** 6 SERVINGS

1. In a large bowl, combine the egg, onion, red pepper, ½ cup mozzarella cheese, ½ cup spaghetti sauce, 2 Tbsp. Parmesan cheese, oats and seasonings. Crumble turkey over mixture and mix well.

2. Coat 6 jumbo muffin cups with cooking spray; fill with turkey mixture. Bake at 350° for 20 minutes; drain.

3. Top each loaf with 1 Tbsp. spaghetti sauce, 2 tsp. mozzarella cheese and ½ tsp. Parmesan. Bake 5-10 minutes longer or until a thermometer reads 165° and cheese is melted. Let stand 5 minutes before removing from pan.

1 MEAT LOAF: 210 cal., 10g fat (4g sat. fat), 105mg chol., 447mg sod., 9g carb. (5g sugars, 2g fiber), 20g pro. **DIABETIC EXCHANGES:** 3 lean meat, ½ starch.

- 1 large egg, lightly beaten
- 1 large onion, finely chopped
- 1 small sweet red pepper, finely chopped
- ¾ cup shredded part-skim mozzarella cheese, divided
- ½ cup plus 6 Tbsp. spaghetti sauce, divided
- 3 Tbsp. grated Parmesan cheese, divided
- 3 Tbsp. quick-cooking oats
- 1 tsp. Italian seasoning
- ¼ tsp. salt
- ¼ tsp. pepper
- 1 lb. lean ground turkey

Save money by making your own marinara sauce. Recipe on p. 313.

SNEAKY TURKEY MEATBALLS

Like most kids, mine refuse to eat certain veggies. In order to get healthy foods into their
diets, I have to be sneaky sometimes. The recipe's veggies give the meatballs a pleasing texture
while providing valuable nutrients — and I'm happy to say that my kids love 'em.
—*Courtney Stultz, Weir, KS*

PREP: 15 MIN. • **BAKE:** 20 MIN. • **MAKES:** 6 SERVINGS

¼ head cauliflower,
  broken into florets
½ cup finely shredded cabbage
1 Tbsp. potato starch or cornstarch
1 Tbsp. balsamic vinegar
1 tsp. sea salt
1 tsp. dried basil
½ tsp. pepper
1 lb. ground turkey
  Optional: Barbecue sauce and
  fresh basil leaves

1. Preheat oven to 400°. Place cauliflower in a food processor; pulse until finely chopped. Transfer to a large bowl. Add the cabbage, potato starch, vinegar, salt, basil and pepper.

2. Add turkey; mix lightly but thoroughly. With an ice cream scoop or with wet hands, shape into 1½-in. balls. Place meatballs on a greased rack in a 15x10x1-in. baking pan. Bake 20-24 minutes or until cooked through. If desired, toss with barbecue sauce and top with basil.

FREEZE OPTION: Freeze cooled meatball mixture in freezer containers. To use, partially thaw in refrigerator overnight. Heat through in a covered saucepan, stirring and adding a little water if necessary. Serve as directed.

2 MEATBALLS: 125 cal., 6g fat (1g sat. fat), 50mg chol., 370mg sod., 4g carb. (1g sugars, 1g fiber), 15g pro. **DIABETIC EXCHANGES:** 2 medium-fat meat.

SHEET-PAN CAESAR CHICKEN & POTATOES

In our area we have an abundance of fresh lemons year-round. When I had a few
extra on hand, I put together a quick marinade and ended up with a really tasty meal that had a
wonderful burst of flavor. I baked it so I could add potatoes, but you can grill the chicken if you prefer.
—*Kallee Krong-Mccreery, Escondido, CA*

PREP: 15 MIN. + MARINATING • **BAKE:** 30 MIN. • **MAKES:** 4 SERVINGS

1. For marinade, in a large bowl, mix lemon juice and dressing; remove 2 Tbsp. mixture for potatoes. Add chicken to remaining marinade; turn to coat. Cover and refrigerate chicken and reserved marinade 4 hours or overnight.

2. Preheat oven to 400°. Place chicken on center of a foil-lined 15x10x1-in. baking pan; discard the chicken marinade. Toss potatoes and carrots with reserved marinade and the seasonings; arrange around chicken.

3. Roast until a thermometer inserted in chicken reads 170°-175° and potatoes are tender, 30-40 minutes.

1 CHICKEN THIGH WITH 1 CUP VEGETABLES: 348 cal., 18g fat (5g sat. fat), 80mg chol., 698mg sod., 20g carb. (4g sugars, 3g fiber), 25g pro.

¼ cup lemon juice
¼ cup Caesar vinaigrette
4 bone-in chicken thighs (about 1½ lbs.)
3 medium red potatoes (about 1¼ lbs.), each cut into 8 wedges
½ lb. medium carrots, cut into 1½-in. pieces
1 tsp. garlic salt
½ tsp. dill weed
¼ tsp. pepper

TERIYAKI CHICKEN THIGHS

Here's a real slow-cooker sensation: Asian-style
chicken and rice. It always goes over big with my family.
Gigi Miller, Stoughton, WI

PREP: 15 MIN. • **COOK:** 4 HOURS • **MAKES:** 8 SERVINGS

1. Place chicken in a 4- or 5-qt. slow cooker. In a small bowl, mix sugar, soy sauce, vinegar, garlic, ginger and pepper; pour over chicken. Cook, covered, on low 4-5 hours or until chicken is tender.

2. Remove chicken to a serving platter; keep warm. Transfer cooking juices to a small saucepan; skim fat. Bring cooking juices to a boil. In a small bowl, mix cornstarch and cold water until smooth; stir into cooking juices. Return to a boil; cook and stir 1-2 minutes or until thickened. Serve with chicken and, if desired, rice.

5 OZ. COOKED CHICKEN WITH ⅓ CUP SAUCE: 342 cal., 12g fat (3g sat. fat), 113mg chol., 958mg sod., 22g carb. (19g sugars, 0 fiber), 33g pro.

3 lbs. boneless skinless
   chicken thighs
¾ cup sugar
¾ cup reduced-sodium soy sauce
⅓ cup cider vinegar
1 garlic clove, minced
¾ tsp. ground ginger
¼ tsp. pepper
4 tsp. cornstarch
4 tsp. cold water
   Hot cooked rice, optional

MY TWO CENTS

*"My teen and tween
sons loved it and
wanted seconds.
I sent the small
amount of leftovers
in school lunches the
next day by request.
This is on the
favorites list."*

—BETH1697, TASTEOFHOME.COM

BUFFALO TURKEY BURGERS

Celery and blue cheese dressing help tame the hot sauce on these juicy burgers. For an even lighter version, pass on the buns and serve the burgers with lettuce leaves, sliced onion and chopped tomato.
—*Mary Pax-Shipley, Bend, OR*

TAKES: 25 MIN. • **MAKES:** 4 SERVINGS

2 Tbsp. Louisiana-style hot sauce, divided
2 tsp. ground cumin
2 tsp. chili powder
2 garlic cloves, minced
½ tsp. salt
⅛ tsp. pepper
1 lb. lean ground turkey
4 whole wheat hamburger buns, split
1 cup shredded lettuce
2 celery ribs, chopped
2 Tbsp. fat-free blue cheese salad dressing

1. In a large bowl, combine 1 Tbsp. hot sauce, cumin, chili powder, garlic, salt and pepper. Add turkey; mix lightly but thoroughly. Shape into four ½-in.-thick patties.

2. In a large nonstick skillet, cook burgers over medium heat 4-6 minutes on each side or until a thermometer reads 165°.

3. Serve burgers on buns with lettuce, celery, salad dressing and the remaining hot sauce.

FREEZE OPTION: Place patties on a waxed paper-lined baking sheet; cover and freeze until firm. Remove from pan and transfer to an airtight container; return to freezer. To use, cook frozen patties as directed, increasing time as necessary for a thermometer to read 165°.

1 BURGER: 312 cal., 12g fat (3g sat. fat), 90mg chol., 734mg sod., 28g carb. (5g sugars, 5g fiber), 24g pro. **DIABETIC EXCHANGES:** 3 lean meat, 2 starch, ½ fat.

SEAFOOD ALFREDO

My guests usually can't believe I prepared this meal myself. The rich, creamy main dish features plenty of seafood flavors with a hint of garlic and lemon. Frozen peas and a jar of Alfredo sauce make it a simple supper that will be requested time and again.
—*Melissa Mosness, Loveland, CO*

TAKES: 20 MIN. • **MAKES:** 6 SERVINGS

1   pkg. (12 oz.) bow tie pasta
2   garlic cloves, minced
2   Tbsp. olive oil
1   pkg. (8 oz.) imitation crabmeat, flaked
1   pkg. (5 oz.) frozen cooked salad shrimp, thawed
1   Tbsp. lemon juice
½   tsp. pepper
1   jar (16 oz.) Alfredo sauce
½   cup frozen peas, thawed
¼   cup grated or shredded Parmesan cheese

1. Cook pasta according to package directions.

2. Meanwhile, in a large skillet, saute garlic in oil until tender. Add the crab, shrimp, lemon juice and pepper. Cook and stir for 1 minute. Add Alfredo sauce and peas. Cook and stir until heated through.

3. Drain pasta; top with the seafood mixture and sprinkle with Parmesan cheese.

1 CUP: 436 cal., 15g fat (7g sat. fat), 74mg chol., 635mg sod., 55g carb. (5g sugars, 3g fiber), 22g pro.

MY TWO CENTS
"This recipe was tasty. It was as if I made it from scratch. I had only a 1-lb. bag of small shrimp, so I used all of that. Will definitely make this again."
—VIRGINIAABBE, TASTEOFHOME.COM

FIRECRACKER GRILLED SALMON

Let this sensational salmon perk up dinner tonight. With a super flavorful glaze that kicks you right in the taste buds, this weeknight dish is anything but boring.
—*Melissa Rogers, Tuscaloosa, AL*

PREP: 20 MIN. + MARINATING • **GRILL:** 5 MIN. • **MAKES:** 4 SERVINGS

1. In a small bowl, combine the first 10 ingredients. Pour ¼ cup marinade into a large resealable container. Add the salmon; seal container and turn to coat salmon. Refrigerate for up to 30 minutes. Cover and refrigerate remaining marinade.

2. Drain salmon, discarding marinade in container. Place salmon, skin side down, on a greased grill rack. Grill, covered, over high heat or broil 3-4 in. from the heat for 5-10 minutes or until fish flakes easily with a fork, basting occasionally with remaining marinade.

1 FILLET: 306 cal., 18g fat (4g sat. fat), 85mg chol., 367mg sod., 4g carb. (3g sugars, 0 fiber), 29g pro. **DIABETIC EXCHANGES:** 5 lean meat, 1 fat.text

2 Tbsp. balsamic vinegar
2 Tbsp. reduced-sodium soy sauce
1 green onion, thinly sliced
1 Tbsp. olive oil
1 Tbsp. maple syrup
2 garlic cloves, minced
1 tsp. ground ginger
1 tsp. crushed red pepper flakes
½ tsp. sesame oil
¼ tsp. salt
4 salmon fillets (6 oz. each)

- SEAFOOD -

CRAB MELT FOR A CROWD

Our family loves seafood, and this recipe is a nice switch from traditional sandwiches.
I've served big slices of it for lunch, for Sunday brunch and as a light dinner with salad.
—*Louise Fauth, Foremost, AB*

TAKES: 30 MIN. • **MAKES:** 8 SERVINGS

1 lb. imitation crabmeat, chopped
½ cup mayonnaise
¼ cup thinly sliced green onions
¼ cup diced celery
2 cups shredded part-skim
   mozzarella cheese
⅛ tsp. salt
⅛ tsp. pepper
1 loaf (1 lb.) unsliced
   French bread, split

1. In a large bowl, combine the crab, mayonnaise, onions and celery. Stir in the cheese, salt and pepper. Spread over bread bottom; replace top.

2. Wrap in a large piece of heavy-duty foil. Place on an ungreased baking sheet. Bake at 400° for 20 minutes or until heated through. Cut into slices.

1 SERVING: 389 cal., 19g fat (6g sat. fat), 34mg chol., 879mg sod., 38g carb. (1g sugars, 2g fiber), 16g pro.

HOMEMADE FISH STICKS

I am a nutritionist and needed a healthy fish fix. Moist inside and crunchy outside,
these are amazing with oven fries or roasted veggies and low-fat homemade tartar sauce.
Jennifer Rowland, Elizabethtown, KY

TAKES: 25 MIN. • **MAKES:** 2 SERVINGS

½ cup dry bread crumbs
½ tsp. salt
½ tsp. paprika
½ tsp. lemon-pepper seasoning
½ cup all-purpose flour
1 large egg, beaten
¾ lb. cod fillets, cut into 1-in. strips
   Butter-flavored cooking spray

1. Preheat oven to 400°. In a shallow bowl, mix bread crumbs and seasonings. Place flour and egg in separate shallow bowls. Dip fish in flour to coat both sides; shake off excess. Dip in egg, then in crumb mixture, patting to help the coating adhere.

2. Place on a baking sheet coated with cooking spray; spritz fish with butter-flavored cooking spray. Bake 10-12 minutes or until fish just begins to flake easily with a fork, turning once.

1 SERVING: 278 cal., 4g fat (1g sat. fat), 129mg chol., 718mg sod., 25g carb. (2g sugars, 1g fiber), 33g pro. **DIABETIC EXCHANGES:** 4 lean meat, 1½ starch.

SPEEDY SALMON PATTIES

When I was a girl growing up on the farm, my mom often fixed these nicely seasoned patties when we were working late in the field. They're also tasty with chopped green peppers added to the mixture.
—*Bonnie Evans, Cameron, NC*

TAKES: 25 MIN. • **MAKES:** 3 SERVINGS

⅓ cup finely chopped onion
1 large egg, beaten
5 saltines, crushed
½ tsp. Worcestershire sauce
¼ tsp. salt
⅛ tsp. pepper
1 can (14¾ oz.) salmon, drained, bones and skin removed
2 tsp. butter

1. In a large bowl, combine the first 6 ingredients. Crumble salmon over mixture and mix well. Shape into 6 patties.

2. In a large skillet over medium heat, fry patties in butter for 3-4 minutes on each side or until set and golden brown.

2 SALMON PATTIES: 288 cal., 15g fat (4g sat. fat), 139mg chol., 1063mg sod., 5g carb. (1g sugars, 0 fiber), 31g pro.

THRIFTY TIP

Canned salmon is a convenient way to include more fish in your diet. If you don't mind the fine pin bones, leave them in to boost the dish's calcium content. Discard the vertebrae.

CAJUN BAKED CATFISH

This well-seasoned fish gets compliments from family and friends whenever I serve it. It's moist and flaky, and the coating is crispy, crunchy and flecked with paprika.

Jim Gales, Milwaukee, WI

TAKES: 25 MIN. • **MAKES:** 2 SERVINGS

1. Preheat oven to 400°. In a shallow bowl, mix the first 6 ingredients.

2. Dip fillets in cornmeal mixture to coat both sides. Place on a baking sheet coated with cooking spray. Sprinkle with paprika.

3. Bake until fish begins to flake easily with a fork, 20-25 minutes.

1 FILLET: 242 cal., 10g fat (2g sat. fat), 94mg chol., 748mg sod., 8g carb. (0 sugars, 1g fiber), 27g pro. **DIABETIC EXCHANGES:** 4 lean meat, ½ starch.

- 2   Tbsp. yellow cornmeal
- 2   tsp. Cajun or blackened seasoning
- ½   tsp. dried thyme
- ½   tsp. dried basil
- ¼   tsp. garlic powder
- ¼   tsp. lemon-pepper seasoning
- 2   catfish or tilapia fillets (6 oz. each)
- ¼   tsp. paprika

PARMESAN BAKED COD

This is a goof-proof way to keep oven-baked cod moist and flavorful.
My mom shared this recipe with me years ago and I've been loving it ever since.
—*Mary Jo Hoppe, Pewaukee, WI*

TAKES: 25 MIN. • **MAKES:** 4 SERVINGS

4   cod fillets (4 oz. each)
⅔   cup mayonnaise
4   green onions, chopped
¼   cup grated Parmesan cheese
1   tsp. Worcestershire sauce

1. Preheat oven to 400°. Place cod in an 8-in. square baking dish coated with cooking spray. Mix remaining ingredients; spread over fillets.

2. Bake, uncovered, until fish just begins to flake easily with a fork, 15-20 minutes.

1 FILLET: 247 cal., 15g fat (2g sat. fat), 57mg chol., 500mg sod., 7g carb. (2g sugars, 0 fiber), 20g pro. **DIABETIC EXCHANGES:** 3 lean meat, 3 fat.

MY TWO CENTS
"I love this recipe! My family asks for it every few weeks. I occasionally add a touch of garlic."
—CAROLNORTH, TASTEOFHOME.COM

QUICK NICOISE SALAD

Like the French, I pack my classic Nicoise salad with veggies, potatoes, tuna and eggs.
Cooking the potatoes and beans together helps the dish come together fast.
—*Valerie Belley, St. Louis, MO*

TAKES: 25 MIN. • **MAKES:** 4 SERVINGS

1. Place potatoes in a large saucepan; add water to cover. Bring to a boil. Reduce heat; cook, uncovered, until tender, 8-10 minutes, adding green beans during the last 3 minutes of cooking. Drain potatoes and beans; immediately drop into ice water. Drain and pat dry.

2. In a small bowl, combine salad dressing, lemon zest and pepper. Divide romaine among 4 plates; arrange potatoes, green beans, eggs, tuna and tomatoes over romaine. Serve with dressing mixture.

1 SERVING: 327 cal., 15g fat (2g sat. fat), 206mg chol., 691mg sod., 27g carb. (7g sugars, 5g fiber), 21g pro. **DIABETIC EXCHANGES:** 3 lean meat, 2 vegetable, 2 fat, 1 starch.

- 1 lb. red potatoes
  (about 2 large), cubed
- ¼ lb. fresh green beans, trimmed
- ½ cup oil and vinegar
  salad dressing
- ½ tsp. grated lemon zest
- ¼ tsp. freshly ground pepper
- 6 cups torn romaine
- 4 hard-boiled large eggs, sliced
- 3 pouches (2½ oz. each)
  light tuna in water
- 2 medium tomatoes, chopped

MAKE IT YOUR OWN

Tasty additions to the salad may include Nicoise, kalamata or other black olives, as well as chopped cucumber for crunch, wax beans for color and rinsed capers for a flavor burst. Choose a simple vinaigrette.

LINGUINE WITH RED CLAM SAUCE

This sensational basil-seasoned clam sauce will shake up your dinner routine.
It's a nice change from typical meat-based pasta sauces.
—*Laura Valdez, Brownsville, TX*

TAKES: 25 MIN • **MAKES:** 4 SERVINGS

2   tsp. minced garlic
2   Tbsp. butter
1½ tsp. olive oil
1   can (15 oz.) tomato sauce
1   can (6½ oz.) chopped
    clams, drained
1   Tbsp. dried parsley flakes
1   Tbsp. dried basil
⅛   tsp. pepper
    Hot cooked linguine

In a large saucepan, saute garlic in butter and oil for 30 seconds. Stir in the tomato sauce, clams, parsley, basil and pepper. Bring to a boil. Reduce heat; cover and simmer for 15 minutes, stirring occasionally. Serve with linguine.

1 SERVING: 115 cal., 7g fat (4g sat. fat), 23mg chol., 739mg sod., 8g carb. (2g sugars, 1g fiber), 5g pro.

SALMON QUICHE

Cooking is something that I've always liked doing. I pore over cookbooks the way other people read novels. This recipe came to me from my mother—it's the kind of recipe you request after just one bite. And unlike some quiches, it's very hearty!
—Deanna Baldwin, Bermuda Dunes, CA

PREP: 15 MIN. • **BAKE:** 1 HOUR • **MAKES:** 8 SERVINGS

1   sheet refrigerated pie crust
1   medium onion, chopped
1   Tbsp. butter
2   cups shredded Swiss cheese
1   can (14¾ oz.) salmon, drained, flaked and cartilage removed
5   large eggs
2   cups half-and-half cream
¼   tsp. salt
   Minced fresh parsley, optional

1. Unroll the crust into a 9-in. pie plate. Line unpricked pie crust with a double thickness of heavy-duty foil. Bake at 450° for 8 minutes. Remove foil; bake 5 minutes longer. Cool on a wire rack.

2. In a small skillet, saute onion in butter until tender. Sprinkle cheese in the crust; top with salmon and onion.

3. In a small bowl, whisk the eggs, cream and salt; pour over salmon mixture. Bake at 350° for 45-50 minutes or until a knife inserted in the center comes out clean. Sprinkle with parsley if desired. Let stand 5 minutes before cutting.

1 PIECE: 448 cal., 29g fat (15g sat. fat), 219mg chol., 610mg sod., 18g carb. (5g sugars, 0 fiber), 26g pro.

OVEN FISH & CHIPS

Enjoy moist, flavorful fish with a coating that's as crunchy and golden
as the deep-fried kind. Plus, the crispy fries are irresistible!
—*Janice Mitchell, Aurora, CO*

PREP: 40 MIN. • **BAKE:** 10 MIN. • **MAKES:** 4 SERVINGS

2   Tbsp. olive oil
¼   tsp. pepper
4   medium baking potatoes
    (1 lb.), peeled

FISH
⅓   cup all-purpose flour
¼   tsp. pepper
¼   cup egg substitute
2   Tbsp. water
⅔   cup crushed cornflakes
1   Tbsp. grated Parmesan cheese
⅛   tsp. cayenne pepper
1   lb. haddock fillets
    Tartar sauce, optional

**Save money by making your own
tartar sauce. Recipe on p. 312.*

1. In a large bowl, combine oil and pepper. Cut potatoes lengthwise into ½-in. strips. Add to oil mixture; toss to coat. Place on a 15x10x1-in. baking pan coated with cooking spray. Bake, uncovered, at 425° for 25-30 minutes or until golden brown and crisp.

2. Meanwhile, combine flour and pepper in a shallow dish. In a second dish, beat egg substitute and water. In a third dish, combine cornflakes, cheese and cayenne. Dredge fish in flour, then dip in egg mixture and roll in crumb mixture.

3. Place on a baking sheet coated with cooking spray. Bake at 425° for 10-15 minutes or until fish flakes easily with a fork. Serve with chips and, if desired, tartar sauce.

1 SERVING: 243 cal., 2g fat (0 sat. fat), 67mg chol., 328mg sod., 28g carb. (0 sugars, 0 fiber), 27g pro. **DIABETIC EXCHANGES:** 3 lean meat, 2 starch.

TUNA NOODLE CUPS

Older kids can get a jump on preparing dinner by stirring up these miniature tuna casseroles. Or serve them for brunch with fresh fruit, a tossed salad and rolls.
—*Marlene Pugh, Fort McMurray, AB*

PREP: 25 MIN • **BAKE:** 30 MIN • **MAKES:** 9 SERVINGS

1. Preheat oven to 350°. In a 6-qt. stockpot, cook egg noodles according to package directions; drain and return to pot. Add tuna, peas and carrots, onion and 1 cup cheese.

2. Whisk together eggs, milk, water and seasonings; toss with noodle mixture. Divide among 18 well-greased muffin cups. Sprinkle with remaining cheese.

3. Bake until heated through, 30-35 minutes. Cool 5 minutes. Loosen edges with a knife before removing from pans.

2 NOODLE CUPS: 316 cal., 14g fat (7g sat. fat), 131mg chol., 549mg sod., 27g carb. (5g sugars, 2g fiber), 21g pro.

8 oz. uncooked medium egg noodles (about 4 cups)
2 cans (5 oz. each) light tuna in water, drained
2 cups frozen peas and carrots (about 10 oz.), thawed
1 small onion, finely chopped
2 cups shredded cheddar cheese, divided
3 large eggs
1 can (12 oz.) evaporated milk
½ cup water
1 tsp. garlic salt
¼ tsp. pepper

FISH SOFT TACOS

My husband and I were cooking together in the kitchen one day and we came up with these tasty fish tacos. The combination of tilapia, cabbage and a hint of cumin is fun. After one bite, everyone's hooked!
—*Carrie Billups, Florence, OR*

TAKES: 25 MIN. • **MAKES:** 5 SERVINGS

4 cups coleslaw mix
⅓ cup tartar sauce
½ tsp. salt
½ tsp. ground cumin
¼ tsp. pepper
1½ lbs. tilapia fillets
2 Tbsp. olive oil
1 Tbsp. lemon juice
10 corn tortillas (6 in.), warmed
  Optional: Shredded cheddar cheese, chopped tomato and sliced avocado

Save money by making your own tartar sauce. Recipe on p. 312.

1. In a large bowl, toss the coleslaw mix, tartar sauce, salt, cumin and pepper; set aside. In a large nonstick skillet, cook tilapia in oil and lemon juice over medium heat for 4-5 minutes on each side or until fish flakes easily with a fork.

2. Place tilapia on tortillas; top with coleslaw mixture. Serve with cheese, tomato and avocado if desired.

2 TACOS: 309 cal., 11g fat (2g sat. fat), 66mg chol., 423mg sod., 26g carb. (4g sugars, 4g fiber), 29g pro. **DIABETIC EXCHANGES:** 4 lean meat, 4 very lean meat, 2 starch, 2 fat.

MY TWO CENTS
"Very easy. I used pico de gallo instead of tartar sauce, and a splash of lime juice."
—SERGIO56, TASTEOFHOME.COM

BROWN SUGAR-GLAZED SALMON

Pop these protein-packed salmon fillets in the oven before whipping up a sweet basting sauce. This tangy entree cooks up in minutes, making it a perfect meal for busy families and unexpected weekend guests.
—*Debra Martin, Belleville, MI*

TAKES: 25 MIN. • **MAKES:** 4 SERVINGS

1. Preheat oven to 425°. Cut salmon into 4 portions; place in a foil-lined 15x10x1-in. pan. Sprinkle with salt and pepper. Roast 10 minutes. Remove from the oven; preheat broiler.

2. In a small saucepan, mix remaining ingredients; bring just to a boil. Brush over salmon. Broil salmon 6 in. from heat until fish just begins to flake easily with a fork, 1-2 minutes.

3 OZ. COOKED FISH: 225 cal., 10g fat (2g sat. fat), 57mg chol., 491mg sod., 11g carb. (10g sugars, 0 fiber), 19g pro. **DIABETIC EXCHANGES:** 3 lean meat, 1 starch.

1   salmon fillet (1 lb.)
¼ tsp. salt
¼ tsp. pepper
3   Tbsp. brown sugar
4   tsp. Dijon mustard
1   Tbsp. reduced-sodium soy sauce
1   tsp. rice vinegar

FEED YOUR FREEZER

Oily fish such as salmon, mackerel and lake trout can be frozen for up to 3 months. If you score salmon on a good sale, wrap the fish in freezer paper or heavy-duty foil, or place it in a freezer container, label it and freeze it. (Lean fish such as cod and tilapia can be frozen for up to 6 months.)

BLACK BEAN SHRIMP SALAD

I lived in Venezuela for several years, so this Caribbean-style salad is a favorite of mine.
I came across the recipe about 10 years ago and changed it to suit my taste.
—*Rosemarie Forcum, Heathsville, VA*

PREP: 15 MIN. ⏐ CHILLING • **MAKES:** 6 SERVINGS

1 lb. cooked shrimp (31-40 per lb.),
   peeled and deveined
1 can (15 oz.) black beans,
   rinsed and drained
1 small green pepper, julienned
1 small onion, thinly sliced
½ cup chopped celery
⅔ cup picante sauce
2 Tbsp. minced fresh cilantro
2 Tbsp. lime juice
2 Tbsp. olive oil
2 Tbsp. honey
½ tsp. salt
⅛ tsp. grated lime zest, optional
6 lettuce leaves
1 cup halved cherry tomatoes

1. In a large bowl, combine the first 5 ingredients.

2. In a small bowl, whisk the picante sauce, cilantro, lime juice, oil, honey, salt and, if desired, lime zest. Pour over shrimp mixture and toss to coat. Cover and refrigerate for at least 2 hours.

3. Using a slotted spoon, spoon onto a lettuce-lined serving platter or lettuce-lined salad plates. Garnish with tomatoes.

¾ CUP: 224 cal., 6g fat (1g sat. fat), 115mg chol., 571mg sod., 22g carb. (9g sugars, 4g fiber), 19g pro. **DIABETIC EXCHANGES:** 2 lean meat, 1 starch, 1 vegetable, 1 fat.

KEEP FISH AT ITS FRESHEST

Fish stays freshest when stored on ice. To keep it ice cold without damaging the fish's texture, place frozen gel packs or blue ice blocks in a container, then top with wrapped fish. Store fish in the meat drawer. Use in a few days. Wash ice packs with hot soapy water before re-use.

BROILED COD

This is the easiest and tastiest fish you'll serve. Even finicky eaters who
think they don't like fish will love the beautiful and flaky results.
—*Kim Russell, North Wales, PA*

TAKES: 30 MIN. • **MAKES:** 2 SERVINGS

¼ cup fat-free
   Italian salad dressing
½ tsp. sugar
⅛ tsp. salt
⅛ tsp. garlic powder
⅛ tsp. curry powder
⅛ tsp. paprika
⅛ tsp. pepper
2 cod fillets (6 oz. each)
2 tsp. butter

1. Preheat broiler. In a shallow bowl, mix first 7 ingredients; add cod, turning
to coat. Let stand 10-15 minutes.

2. Place fillets on a greased rack of a broiler pan; discard the remaining
marinade. Broil 3-4 in. from heat until fish just begins to flake easily with
a fork, 10-12 minutes. Top with butter.

1 FILLET: 168 cal., 5g fat (3g sat. fat), 75mg chol., 365mg sod., 2g carb. (2g sugars,
0 fiber), 27g pro. **DIABETIC EXCHANGES:** 4 lean meat, 1 fat.

BLACK BEAN & SWEET POTATO RICE BOWLS

I have three hungry boys in my house, so dinners need to be quick and filling, and it helps to get in some veggies too. This one is a favorite because it's hearty and fun to tweak with different ingredients.
—*Kim Van Dunk, Caldwell, NJ*

TAKES: 30 MIN. • **MAKES:** 4 SERVINGS

¾ cup uncooked long grain rice
¼ tsp. garlic salt
1½ cups water
3 Tbsp. olive oil, divided
1 large sweet potato,
 peeled and diced
1 medium red onion,
 finely chopped
4 cups chopped fresh kale
 (tough stems removed)
1 can (15 oz.) black beans,
 rinsed and drained
2 Tbsp. sweet chili sauce
 Optional: Lime wedges and
 additional sweet chili sauce

1. Place rice, garlic salt and water in a large saucepan; bring to a boil. Reduce heat; simmer, covered, until water is absorbed and rice is tender, 15-20 minutes. Remove from heat; let stand 5 minutes.

2. Meanwhile, in a large skillet, heat 2 Tbsp. oil over medium-high heat; saute sweet potato 8 minutes. Add onion; cook and stir until potato is tender, 4-6 minutes. Add kale; cook and stir until tender, 3-5 minutes. Stir in beans; heat through.

3. Gently stir 2 Tbsp. chili sauce and remaining oil into rice; add to the potato mixture. If desired, serve with lime wedges and additional chili sauce.

2 CUPS: 435 cal., 11g fat (2g sat. fat), 0 chol., 405mg sod., 74g carb. (15g sugars, 8g fiber), 10g pro.

CHEESY VEGGIE LASAGNA

This is my daughter-in-law's recipe. It's tasty and a little different from usual lasagna recipes. You won't even miss the meat!
—Alyce Wyman, Pembina, ND

PREP: 30 MIN. • **BAKE:** 40 MIN. + STANDING • **MAKES:** 2 LASAGNAS (9 SERVINGS EACH)

18 uncooked lasagna noodles
3 large eggs
2 cartons (15 oz. each)
   reduced-fat ricotta cheese
4 tsp. dried parsley flakes
2 tsp. dried basil
2 tsp. dried oregano
1 tsp. pepper
8 cups garden-style
   spaghetti sauce
4 cups shredded part-skim
   mozzarella cheese
2 pkg. (16 oz. each) frozen
   cut green beans or 8 cups
   cut fresh green beans
⅔ cup grated Parmesan cheese

1. Cook noodles according to package directions. Meanwhile, in a small bowl, whisk the eggs, ricotta cheese, parsley, basil, oregano and pepper; set aside.

2. In each of two 13x9-in. baking dishes coated with cooking spray, spread 1 cup spaghetti sauce. Drain noodles; place 3 noodles over spaghetti sauce in each dish.

3. Layer each with a quarter of the ricotta mixture, 1 cup spaghetti sauce, 1 cup mozzarella cheese, 3 lasagna noodles and half the green beans. Top each with remaining ricotta mixture and 1 cup spaghetti sauce. Layer with remaining lasagna noodles, spaghetti sauce and mozzarella cheese. Sprinkle Parmesan cheese over each.

4. Cover and freeze 1 casserole for up to 3 months. Bake remaining lasagna, uncovered, at 375° for 40-45 minutes or until bubbly and edges are lightly browned. Let stand for 10 minutes before serving.

TO USE FROZEN LASAGNA: Thaw in the refrigerator overnight. Remove from the refrigerator 30 minutes before baking. Cover and bake at 375° for 1¼-1½ hours or until bubbly. Let stand for 10 minutes before serving.

1 PIECE: 327 cal., 11g fat (5g sat. fat), 61mg chol., 703mg sod., 39g carb. (13g sugars, 4g fiber), 18g pro. **DIABETIC EXCHANGES:** 2 starch, 2 vegetable, 2 medium-fat meat.

MUSHROOM & BROWN RICE HASH WITH POACHED EGGS

I made my mother's famous roast beef hash healthier by using cremini mushrooms
instead of beef and brown rice instead of potatoes. It's ideal for a light main dish.
—Lily Julow, Lawrenceville, GA

TAKES: 30 MIN. • **MAKES:** 4 SERVINGS

2 Tbsp. olive oil
1 lb. sliced baby portobello
   mushrooms
½ cup chopped sweet onion
1 pkg. (8.8 oz.) ready-to-serve
   brown rice
1 large carrot, grated
2 green onions, thinly sliced
½ tsp. salt
¼ tsp. pepper
¼ tsp. caraway seeds
4 large eggs

1. In a large skillet, heat oil over medium-high heat; saute mushrooms until lightly browned, 5-7 minutes. Add sweet onion; cook 1 minute. Add rice and carrot; cook and stir until vegetables are tender, 4-5 minutes. Stir in green onions, salt, pepper and caraway seeds; heat through.

2. Meanwhile, place 2-3 in. water in a large saucepan or skillet with high sides. Bring to a boil; adjust heat to maintain a gentle simmer. Break cold eggs, 1 at a time, into a small bowl; holding bowl close to surface of water, slip each egg into the water.

3. Cook, uncovered, until whites are completely set and yolks begin to thicken but are not hard, 3-5 minutes. Using a slotted spoon, lift eggs out of water. Serve over rice mixture.

1 SERVING: 282 cal., 13g fat (3g sat. fat), 186mg chol., 393mg sod., 26g carb. (4g sugars, 3g fiber), 13g pro. **DIABETIC EXCHANGES:** 1½ starch, 1½ fat, 1 medium-fat meat.

SAVE SOME CASH

Ready-to-serve rice shaves 40 minutes or more off prep time. But if you plan ahead with homemade already-cooked rice, you'll save some serious cash (and cut down on sodium in the bargain). Instead of using packaged rice, sub in 2 cups cooked brown rice (made from ⅔ cup uncooked rice and 1⅓ cups water).

CARIBBEAN QUESADILLAS

People say the sweet potato in my quesadillas makes them think of the flavor of Thanksgiving.
Often I mix and refrigerate the filling ahead, so it takes no time to layer the tortillas.
—*Flori Christensen, Bloomington, IN*

TAKES: 25 MIN. • **MAKES:** 6 SERVINGS

1 large sweet potato,
 peeled and diced
1 medium onion, chopped
½ to 1 tsp. pumpkin pie spice
2 tsp. canola oil
2 garlic cloves, minced
2 cans (15 oz. each) black beans,
 rinsed and drained
½ cup chicken broth
12 flour tortillas (8 in.)
1½ cups shredded
 Monterey Jack cheese
1 can (4 oz.) chopped green chiles
 Sour cream and salsa

1. Place sweet potato in a microwave-safe dish. Cover and microwave on high for 5 minutes or until tender.

2. Meanwhile, in a large skillet, saute onion and pumpkin pie spice in oil until onion is tender. Add garlic; cook 1 minute longer. Stir in beans and broth. Bring to a boil. Reduce heat; simmer, uncovered, for 3 minutes or until thickened. Mash beans slightly with a fork. Stir in sweet potato. Cook until heated through.

3. Sprinkle bean mixture over 1 side of 6 tortillas. Top each with ¼ cup cheese and 1 rounded Tbsp. chiles. Top each with a remaining tortilla. Cook on a griddle over low heat for 1-2 minutes on each side or until cheese is melted.

4. Cut into wedges; serve with sour cream and salsa.

1 SERVING: 550 cal., 19g fat (8g sat. fat), 35mg chol., 1017mg sod., 73g carb. (6g sugars, 5g fiber), 21g pro.

GRILLED BEAN BURGERS

These juicy veggie patties have major flavor with cumin, garlic and a little chili powder.
They can hold their own against any veggie burger you'd buy at the supermarket.
—*Marguerite Shaeffer, Sewell, NJ*

PREP: 25 MIN. • **GRILL:** 10 MIN. • **MAKES:** 8 SERVINGS

1. In a large nonstick skillet, heat oil over medium-high heat; saute onion 2 minutes. Add garlic; cook and stir 1 minute. Stir in carrot and spices; cook and stir until carrot is tender, 2-3 minutes. Remove from heat.

2. In a large bowl, mash pinto and black beans using a potato masher. Stir in mustard, soy sauce, ketchup and carrot mixture. Add oats, mixing well. Shape into eight 3½-in. patties.

3. Place burgers on an oiled grill rack over medium heat or on a greased rack of a broiler pan. Grill, covered, or broil 4 in. from heat until lightly browned and heated through, 4-5 minutes per side. Serve on buns with lettuce and salsa.

1 BURGER: 305 cal., 5g fat (1g sat. fat), 0 chol., 736mg sod., 54g carb. (8g sugars, 10g fiber), 12g pro. **DIABETIC EXCHANGES:** 3½ starch, 1 lean meat.

1 Tbsp. olive oil
1 large onion, finely chopped
4 garlic cloves, minced
1 medium carrot, shredded
1 to 2 tsp. chili powder
1 tsp. ground cumin
¼ tsp. pepper
1 can (15 oz.) pinto beans,
  rinsed and drained
1 can (15 oz.) black beans,
  rinsed and drained
2 Tbsp. Dijon mustard
2 Tbsp. reduced-sodium soy sauce
1 Tbsp. ketchup
1½ cups quick-cooking oats
8 whole wheat
  hamburger buns, split
8 lettuce leaves
½ cup salsa

MY TWO CENTS
*"I love these burgers!
I like to chop up a can
of water chestnuts
and add them to the
burgers, and then
I broil them."*
—FTG09, TASTEOFHOME.COM

51

CHEESY SUMMER SQUASH FLATBREADS

When you want a meatless meal with Mediterranean style, these flatbreads
smothered with squash, hummus and mozzarella deliver the goods.
—*Matthew Hass, Ellison Bay, WI*

TAKES: 30 MIN. • **MAKES:** 4 SERVINGS

3 small yellow summer squash,
  sliced ¼ in. thick
1 Tbsp. olive oil
½ tsp. salt
2 cups fresh baby spinach,
  coarsely chopped
2 naan flatbreads
⅓ cup roasted red pepper hummus
1 carton (8 oz.) fresh mozzarella
  cheese pearls
  Pepper

*Save money by making your own
hummus. Recipe on p. 311.*

1. Preheat oven to 425°. Toss the squash with oil and salt; spread evenly in a
15x10x1-in. baking pan. Roast until tender, 8-10 minutes. Transfer to a bowl; stir
in spinach.

2. Place naan on a baking sheet; spread with hummus. Top with squash mixture
and cheese. Bake on a lower oven rack just until cheese is melted, 4-6 minutes.
Sprinkle with pepper.

½ TOPPED FLATBREAD: 332 cal., 20g fat (9g sat. fat), 47mg chol., 737mg sod.,
24g carb. (7g sugars, 3g fiber), 15g pro.

GARDEN VEGETABLE GNOCCHI

When we go meatless, we toss gnocchi (my husband's favorite) with veggies
and a dab of prepared pesto. I also use zucchini in this 30-minute dish.
—*Elisabeth Larsen, Pleasant Grove, UT*

TAKES: 30 MIN. • **MAKES:** 4 SERVINGS

1. Preheat oven to 450°. In a greased 15x10x1-in. baking pan, toss vegetables with oil, salt and pepper. Roast 18-22 minutes or until tender, stirring once.

2. Meanwhile, in a large saucepan, cook gnocchi according to package directions. Drain and return to pan.

3. Stir in roasted vegetables, Alfredo sauce and pesto. If desired, sprinkle with fresh basil.

1½ CUPS: 402 cal., 14g fat (4g sat. fat), 17mg chol., 955mg sod., 57g carb. (12g sugars, 5g fiber), 13g pro.

- 2 medium yellow summer squash, sliced
- 1 medium sweet red pepper, chopped
- 8 oz. sliced fresh mushrooms
- 1 Tbsp. olive oil
- ¼ tsp. salt
- ¼ tsp. pepper
- 1 pkg. (16 oz.) potato gnocchi
- ½ cup Alfredo sauce
- ¼ cup prepared pesto
  Chopped fresh basil, optional

*Save money by making your
own pesto. Recipe on p. 309.*

BAKED RAMEN FRITTATA

A wonderful source of low-cost protein, eggs are an ideal way to liven up
any meal on a budget. If you enjoy egg foo yong, you're sure to like this recipe.
—*Edna Hoffman, Hobron, IN*

PREP: 35 MIN. • **BAKE:** 10 MIN. • **MAKES:** 6 SERVINGS

2 pkg. (3 oz. each) ramen noodles
½ cup thinly sliced celery
2 tsp. canola oil
1 pkg. (8 oz.) sliced
   fresh mushrooms
4 Tbsp. green onions,
   thinly sliced, divided
2 Tbsp. minced fresh gingerroot
6 large eggs
1 tsp. sesame oil
½ tsp. sugar
½ tsp. salt
2 Tbsp. reduced-sodium soy sauce

1. Discard seasoning packet from ramen noodles or save for another use. Cook noodles according to package directions. Drain and rinse in cold water; transfer to a bowl and set aside.

2. Meanwhile, in a large nonstick ovenproof skillet over medium heat, cook the celery in canola oil for 1 minute. Stir in the mushrooms, 2 Tbsp. green onions and ginger; cook and stir for 7 minutes or until mushrooms are lightly browned. Stir into noodles.

3. Whisk the eggs, sesame oil, sugar and salt. Stir into noodle mixture; spread into an even layer in the skillet. Cook on medium for 2 minutes.

4. Bake, uncovered, at 350° for 10-12 minutes or until set. Cut into wedges. Sprinkle with remaining green onions. Drizzle with soy sauce.

1 PIECE: 237 cal., 12g fat (5g sat. fat), 186mg chol., 570mg sod., 21g carb. (2g sugars, 1g fiber), 11g pro. **DIABETIC EXCHANGES:** 1½ starch, 1 medium-fat meat, ½ fat.

TOMATO & AVOCADO SANDWICHES

I'm a vegetarian, and this is a tasty, quick and healthy lunch I could eat for every meal. At my house, we call these sandwiches HATS: hummus, avocado, tomato and shallots. They're all ingredients I almost always have on hand.
—Sarah Jaraha, Moorestown, NJ

TAKES: 10 MIN. • **MAKES:** 2 SERVINGS

½ medium ripe avocado, peeled and mashed
4 slices whole wheat bread, toasted
1 medium tomato, sliced
2 Tbsp. finely chopped shallot
¼ cup hummus

Save money by making your own hummus. Recipe on p. 311.

Spread avocado over 2 slices of toast. Top with tomato and shallot. Spread hummus over remaining toast slices; place on top of avocado toast, facedown on top of tomato layer.

1 SANDWICH: 278 cal., 11g fat (2g sat. fat), 0 chol., 379mg sod., 35g carb. (6g sugars, 9g fiber), 11g pro. **DIABETIC EXCHANGES:** 2 starch, 2 fat.

MY TWO CENTS

"I knew I'd love these when I first saw the picture. I made homemade hummus so I could season it as I wanted. Before putting the sandwich together, I sprinkled everything seasoning on it. YUM. Will definitely make these again and again."
—MS11145, TASTEOFHOME.COM

SPRINGTIME ASPARAGUS PIZZA

Here's a pizza that celebrates spring's best. A chewy crust is topped with a blend of mozzarella and feta cheeses, fresh asparagus spears and even anchovy fillets if you like.
—*Deena Prichep, Portland, OR*

PREP: 20 MIN. • **BAKE:** 10 MIN. • **MAKES:** 8 SERVINGS

1 tsp. cornmeal
1 lb. prepared pizza dough, room temperature
1 cup shredded part-skim mozzarella cheese
½ cup crumbled feta cheese
¾ lb. fresh asparagus, trimmed and cut into 2-in. pieces
2 tsp. grated lemon zest
¼ tsp. crushed red pepper flakes

Save money by making your own pizza dough. Recipe on p. 316.

1. Grease a large baking sheet; sprinkle with cornmeal. Roll out dough into a 15-in. circle; transfer to prepared baking sheet.

2. Sprinkle crust with mozzarella and feta cheeses; top with asparagus. Bake at 450° until crust is golden and cheese is melted, 10-15 minutes. Sprinkle with lemon zest and red pepper flakes.

1 PIECE: 227 cal., 6g fat (2g sat. fat), 15mg chol., 600mg sod., 29g carb. (3g sugars, 3g fiber), 12g pro.

SLOW-COOKED STUFFED PEPPERS

*My favorite kitchen appliance is the slow cooker, and I use mine
more than anyone else I know. Here's a tasty good-for-you dish.*
—Michelle Gurnsey, Lincoln, NE

PREP: 15 MIN. • **COOK:** 3 HOURS • **MAKES:** 4 SERVINGS

1. Cut and discard tops from peppers; remove seeds. In a large bowl, mix beans, cheese, salsa, onion, corn, rice, chili powder and cumin; spoon into peppers. Place in a 5-qt. slow cooker coated with cooking spray.

2. Cook, covered, on low until peppers are tender and filling is heated through, 3-4 hours. If desired, serve with sour cream.

1 STUFFED PEPPER: 317 cal., 10g fat (5g sat. fat), 30mg chol., 565mg sod., 43g carb. (6g sugars, 8g fiber), 15g pro. **DIABETIC EXCHANGES:** 2 starch, 2 vegetable, 2 lean meat, 1 fat.

4   medium sweet red peppers
1   can (15 oz.) black beans,
     rinsed and drained
1   cup shredded pepper jack cheese
¾   cup salsa
1   small onion, chopped
½   cup frozen corn
⅓   cup uncooked converted
     long grain rice
1¼   tsp. chili powder
½   tsp. ground cumin
     Reduced-fat sour cream, optional

CHEESE MANICOTTI

This is the first meal I ever cooked for my husband, and all these years later he still enjoys my manicotti!
—*Joan Hallford, North Richland Hills, TX*

PREP: 25 MIN. • **BAKE:** 1 HOUR • **MAKES:** 7 SERVINGS

1   carton (15 oz.) reduced-fat ricotta cheese
1   small onion, finely chopped
1   large egg, lightly beaten
2   Tbsp. minced fresh parsley
½   tsp. pepper
¼   tsp. salt
1   cup shredded part-skim mozzarella cheese, divided
1   cup grated Parmesan cheese, divided
4   cups marinara sauce
½   cup water
1   pkg. (8 oz.) manicotti shells
    Additional parsley, optional

Save money by making your own marinara sauce. Recipe on p. 313.

1. Preheat oven to 350°. In a small bowl, mix the first 6 ingredients; stir in ½ cup mozzarella cheese and ½ cup Parmesan cheese. In another bowl, mix marinara sauce and water; spread ¾ cup sauce onto bottom of a 13x9-in. baking dish coated with cooking spray. Fill uncooked manicotti shells with ricotta mixture; arrange over sauce. Top with remaining sauce.

2. Bake, covered, 50 minutes or until pasta is tender. Uncover; sprinkle with remaining ½ cup mozzarella and ½ cup Parmesan. Bake 10-15 minutes longer or until cheese is melted. If desired, top with additional parsley.

2 STUFFED MANICOTTI: 361 cal., 13g fat (6g sat. fat), 64mg chol., 1124mg sod., 41g carb. (12g sugars, 4g fiber), 19g pro.

READY WHEN YOU ARE

This recipe can be assembled and refrigerated for up to 3 days; just remove from the fridge 30 minutes before baking as directed. Manicotti can also be assembled and frozen for up to 2 months. To use, partially thaw in the refrigerator overnight. Remove from the fridge 30 minutes before baking. Bake as directed, increasing the time as needed until a thermometer inserted in the center reads 165°.

5i
POLENTA CHILI CASSEROLE

This delicious vegetarian bake combines spicy chili, mixed veggies and homemade polenta. It's so hearty that no one seems to miss the meat.
—*Dan Kelmenson, West Bloomfield, MI*

PREP: 20 MIN. • **BAKE:** 35 MIN. + STANDING • **MAKES:** 8 SERVINGS

1. Preheat oven to 350°. In a large heavy saucepan, bring water and salt to a boil. Reduce heat to a gentle boil; slowly whisk in cornmeal. Cook and stir with a wooden spoon until polenta is thickened and pulls away cleanly from side of pan, 15-20 minutes.

2. Remove from heat. Stir in ¼ cup cheddar cheese until melted.

3. Spread into a 13x9-in. baking dish coated with cooking spray. Bake, uncovered, 20 minutes. Meanwhile, heat chili according to package directions.

4. Spread vegetables over polenta; top with chili. Sprinkle with the remaining cheese. Bake until cheese is melted, 12-15 minutes longer. Let stand 10 minutes before serving.

1 SERVING: 397 cal., 12g fat (6g sat. fat), 57mg chol., 922mg sod., 49g carb. (7g sugars, 7g fiber), 21g pro.

- 4 cups water
- ½ tsp. salt
- 1¼ cups yellow cornmeal
- 2 cups shredded cheddar cheese, divided
- 3 cans (15 oz. each) vegetarian chili with beans
- 1 pkg. (16 oz.) frozen mixed vegetables, thawed and well drained

ROASTED VEGGIE QUESADILLAS

I am always looking for recipes that will encourage children to eat vegetables, and this
one has been a huge success. You can also use other vegetables, such as mushrooms, eggplant,
asparagus and broccoli. Just remember to roast your vegetables before making the quesadillas.
—*Kathy Carlan, Canton, GA*

PREP: 40 MIN. • **COOK:** 5 MIN./BATCH • **MAKES:** 8 SERVINGS

1. In a large bowl, combine the first 9 ingredients. Transfer to a 15x10x1-in. baking pan. Bake at 425°until potatoes are tender, 24-28 minutes.

2. In a small bowl, combine cheeses. Spread ⅓ cup vegetable mixture over half of each tortilla. Sprinkle with ¼ cup cheese; fold tortillas to close. Cook in a greased cast-iron skillet or griddle over low heat until cheese is melted, 1-2 minutes on each side.

1 QUESADILLA: 279 cal., 12g fat (4g sat. fat), 18mg chol., 479mg sod., 30g carb. (4g sugars, 3g fiber), 12g pro. **DIABETIC EXCHANGES:** 2 starch, 1 medium-fat meat, 1 fat.

2 medium red potatoes,
   quartered and sliced
1 medium zucchini,
   quartered and sliced
1 medium sweet red pepper, sliced
1 small onion, chopped
2 Tbsp. olive oil
1 garlic clove, minced
½ tsp. salt
½ tsp. dried oregano
¼ tsp. pepper
1 cup shredded part-skim
   mozzarella cheese
1 cup shredded reduced-fat
   cheddar cheese
8 whole wheat tortillas (8 in.)

MY TWO CENTS
*"Five stars. I served
the quesadillas with
black beans and rice."*
—ORBS, TASTEOFHOME.COM

EASY PESTO PIZZA

We kneaded basil, oregano and Parmesan cheese into packaged bread dough for this full-flavored crust. Purchased pesto sauce keeps it big on taste and convenience.
—Taste of Home *Test Kitchen*

PREP: 20 MIN • **BAKE:** 20 MIN • **MAKES:** 8 SERVINGS

1 loaf (1 lb.) frozen
  bread dough, thawed
½ cup shredded
  Parmesan cheese, divided
½ tsp. dried basil
½ tsp. dried oregano
¼ cup prepared pesto
1 cup sliced fresh mushrooms
1 cup shredded part-skim
  mozzarella cheese

*Save money by making your own
pizza dough and pesto. Recipes on
pp. 316 and 309, respectively.*

1. Preheat oven to 425°. Place dough on a lightly floured surface; let rest for 10 minutes. Knead in ¼ cup cheese, the basil and the oregano. Roll into a 12-in. circle; place on a greased 14-in. pizza pan. Prick with a fork. Bake 10 minutes.

2. Spread pesto sauce over the crust. Sprinkle with mushrooms, mozzarella cheese and the remaining Parmesan cheese. Bake pizza until golden brown, 8-10 minutes.

1 PIECE: 259 cal., 11g fat (4g sat. fat), 17mg chol., 513mg sod., 31g carb. (3g sugars, 2g fiber), 12g pro.

ITALIAN HERB-LENTIL PATTIES WITH MOZZARELLA

My family has requested this meatless recipe over and
over again. It is simple to prepare and even meat lovers like it.
—Geraldine Lucas, Oldsmar, FL

PREP: 50 MIN. • **COOK:** 10 MIN./BATCH • **MAKES:** 10 SERVINGS

1. Cook lentils according to package directions; drain and cool slightly.

2. In a large bowl, combine eggs and seasonings; stir in cooked lentils and oatmeal. Shape into ten ¾-in.-thick patties.

3. In a large nonstick skillet, heat 1 Tbsp. oil over medium heat. Cook patties in batches, 4-6 minutes on each side or until golden brown and a thermometer reads 160°, adding additional oil as needed. Top with cheese; cook 1-2 minutes longer or until cheese is melted. If desired, serve with marinara sauce.

1 PATTY: 416 cal., 12g fat (4g sat. fat), 74mg chol., 517mg sod., 54g carb. (2g sugars, 9g fiber), 26g pro.

3   cups dried lentils, rinsed
3   large eggs, lightly beaten
1   Tbsp. dried minced onion
1   Tbsp. dried parsley flakes
1   tsp. dried basil
1   tsp. salt
½   tsp. dried thyme
¼   tsp. pepper
2   cups uncooked instant oatmeal
2   Tbsp. canola oil
10 slices part-skim mozzarella
    cheese or provolone cheese
    Marinara sauce, warmed,
    optional

*Save money by making your own
marinara sauce. Recipe on p. 313.*

SMALL BUT MIGHTY

Ounce for ounce, lentils have
as much protein as steak—and
they cost only a fraction of the
price! The fiber-rich legumes
contain 90% less fat
than steak too.

SPINACH BURRITOS

I made up this recipe a couple of years ago after trying a similar dish in a restaurant.
Our oldest son tells me these burritos are awesome! Plus, they're easy and inexpensive.
—Dolores Zornow, Poynette, WI

PREP: 20 MIN. • **BAKE:** 20 MIN. • **MAKES:** 6 SERVINGS

½   cup chopped onion
2   garlic cloves, minced
2   tsp. butter
1   pkg. (10 oz.) frozen
      chopped spinach,
      thawed and squeezed dry
⅛   tsp. pepper
6   flour tortillas (10 in.), warmed
¾   cup picante sauce, divided
2   cups shredded reduced-fat
      cheddar cheese, divided

1. In a large skillet, saute onion and garlic in butter until tender. Add spinach and pepper; cook for 2-3 minutes or until heated through.

2. Place about 3 Tbsp. mixture off center on each tortilla; top with 1 Tbsp. picante sauce and 2 Tbsp. cheese. Fold sides and ends over filling and roll up.

3. Place seam side down in a 13x9-in. baking dish coated with cooking spray. Top with remaining picante sauce and cheese. Bake, uncovered, at 350° for 20-25 minutes or until sauce is bubbly and cheese is melted.

1 BURRITO: 382 cal., 15g fat (8g sat. fat), 30mg chol., 1049mg sod., 42g carb. (5g sugars, 4g fiber), 19g pro.

CHAPTER 5

SIDES, SALADS & BREADS

A memorable menu just isn't complete without on-the-side sensations that complement the main course. Here you'll find an economical array of veggies, salads, beans, breads and more.

QUICK AMBROSIA

I mix in a little coconut and just enough marshmallows so it tastes like the creamy ambrosia I grew up with. Now everyone in my home loves it too.
—*Trisha Kruse, Eagle, ID*

TAKES: 10 MIN. • **MAKES:** 6 SERVINGS

1   can (8¼ oz.) fruit cocktail, drained
1   can (8 oz.) unsweetened pineapple chunks, drained
1   cup green grapes
1   cup seedless red grapes
1   cup miniature marshmallows
1   medium banana, sliced
¾   cup vanilla yogurt
½   cup sweetened shredded coconut

In a large bowl, combine all ingredients. Chill until serving.

¾ CUP: 191 cal., 4g fat (3g sat. fat), 2mg chol., 48mg sod., 40g carb. (34g sugars, 2g fiber), 3g pro.

MY TWO CENTS
"Very simple and very good! My family eats it up every time I make it. It has become a staple in our house. I omit the fruit cocktail (not a fan) and add apples and whatever fresh fruit I may have on hand. Wonderful!"
—NEWCOUNTRYWIFE, TASTEOFHOME.COM

ITALIAN DROP BISCUITS

I had been making garlic cheese biscuits for years before I tried spicing them up with some green chiles. These biscuits go well with soups as well as Mexican and Italian foods.
—LaDonna Reed, Ponca City, OK

TAKES: 20 MIN. • **MAKES:** 1½ DOZEN

2 cups biscuit/baking mix
1 cup shredded cheddar cheese
½ cup cold water
2 Tbsp. chopped green chiles
¼ cup butter, melted
1 tsp. dried parsley flakes
½ tsp. Italian seasoning
¼ tsp. garlic powder

Save money by making your own biscuit/baking mix. Recipe on p. 304.

1. In a large bowl, combine the biscuit mix, cheese, water and chiles just until moistened. Drop by heaping tablespoonfuls onto a greased baking sheet.

2. Bake at 450° for 8-10 minutes or until golden brown. In a small bowl, combine butter, parsley, Italian seasoning and garlic powder; brush over warm biscuits.

1 BISCUIT: 99 cal., 6g fat (3g sat. fat), 13mg chol., 235mg sod., 9g carb. (0 sugars, 0 fiber), 2g pro.

GARLIC-BUTTERED GREEN BEANS

These dressed-up beans are simple to make but look and taste special.
They're a perfect side dish for nearly any meal.
—*Adeline Piscitelli, Sayreville, N.J*

TAKES: 15 MIN. • **MAKES:** 6 SERVINGS

1. Place green beans in a large saucepan; cover with water. Bring to a boil; cover and cook until crisp-tender, 8-10 minutes.

2. Meanwhile, in a large skillet, saute the mushrooms in butter until tender, 2-3 minutes. Add onion powder and garlic powder. Drain beans; add to skillet and toss. Season with salt and pepper.

¾ **CUP:** 131 cal., 12g fat (7g sat. fat), 31mg chol., 97mg sod., 7g carb. (2g sugars, 3g fiber), 2g pro.

1 lb. fresh or frozen green beans
½ cup sliced fresh mushrooms
6 Tbsp. butter, cubed
2 to 3 tsp. onion powder
1 to 1½ tsp. garlic powder
   Salt and pepper to taste

CINNAMON SWIRL QUICK BREAD

While cinnamon bread is a natural for breakfast, we love it any time of the day.
This one is a nice twist on traditional cinnamon swirl yeast breads.
—Helen Richardson, Shelbyville, MI

PREP: 15 MIN. • **BAKE:** 45 MIN. + COOLING • **MAKES:** 16 PIECES

2   cups all-purpose flour
1½ cups sugar, divided
1   tsp. baking soda
½   tsp. salt
1   cup buttermilk
1   large egg
¼   cup canola oil
3   tsp. ground cinnamon

GLAZE
¼   cup confectioners' sugar
1½ to 2 tsp. 2% milk

1. Preheat oven to 350°. In a large bowl, combine flour, 1 cup sugar, baking soda and salt. Combine buttermilk, egg and oil; stir into dry ingredients just until moistened. In a small bowl, combine cinnamon and remaining ½ cup sugar.

2. Grease the bottom only of a 9x5-in. loaf pan. Pour half the batter into pan; sprinkle with half the cinnamon sugar. Carefully spread with remaining batter and sprinkle with remaining cinnamon sugar; cut through batter with a knife to swirl.

3. Bake until a toothpick inserted in center comes out clean, 45-50 minutes. Cool 10 minutes before removing from pan to a wire rack to cool completely. For the glaze, combine confectioners' sugar and enough milk to reach desired consistency; drizzle over loaf.

NOTE: To substitute for 1 cup buttermilk, use 1 Tbsp. white vinegar or lemon juice plus enough milk to measure 1 cup. Stir, then let stand 5 minutes. Or, use 1 cup plain yogurt or 1¾ tsp. cream of tartar plus 1 cup milk.

1 PIECE: 179 cal., 4g fat (1g sat. fat), 14mg chol., 173mg sod., 34g carb. (21g sugars, 1g fiber), 3g pro.

(5i) MEXICAN STREET CORN BAKE

We discovered Mexican street corn at a festival. This easy one-pan version
saves on prep and cleanup. Every August I freeze a lot of our own fresh sweet corn
and then I use that in this recipe, but store-bought corn works just as well.
—*Erin Wright, Wallace, KS*

PREP: 10 MIN. • **BAKE:** 35 MIN. • **MAKES:** 6 SERVINGS

1. Preheat oven to 350°. Mix the first 5 ingredients and 4 Tbsp. green onions; transfer to a greased 1½-qt. baking dish. Sprinkle with cheese.

2. Bake, covered, 20 minutes. Uncover; bake until bubbly and lightly browned, 15-20 minutes longer. Sprinkle with remaining green onions. If desired, serve with lime wedges.

⅔ CUP: 391 cal., 30g fat (5g sat. fat), 8mg chol., 423mg sod., 30g carb. (4g sugars, 3g fiber), 6g pro.

- 6 cups frozen corn (about 30 oz.), thawed and drained
- 1 cup mayonnaise
- 1 tsp. ground chipotle pepper
- ¼ tsp. salt
- ¼ tsp. pepper
- 6 Tbsp. chopped green onions, divided
- ½ cup grated Parmesan cheese
  Lime wedges, optional

CARROT RAISIN SALAD

This traditional salad is one of my mother-in-law's favorites. It's fun to eat because of the crunchy texture, and the raisins give it a slightly sweet flavor. Plus, I love how easy it is to prepare.
—Denise Baumert, Dalhart, TX

TAKES: 10 MIN. • **MAKES:** 8 SERVINGS

Mix the first 4 ingredients. Stir in enough milk to reach desired consistency. Refrigerate until serving.

½ CUP: 122 cal., 5g fat (1g sat. fat), 1mg chol., 76mg sod., 19g carb. (14g sugars, 2g fiber), 1g pro. **DIABETIC EXCHANGES:** 1 vegetable, 1 fat, ½ starch, ½ fruit.

4 cups shredded carrots
¾ to 1½ cups raisins
¼ cup mayonnaise
2 Tbsp. sugar
2 to 3 Tbsp. 2% milk

MY TWO CENTS
"Wonderful use of raw carrots. A different take on a salad side. I made it as is; next time I may add some chopped pecans or walnuts for more crunch."

—JGA2595176, TASTEOFHOME.COM

KIWI-STRAWBERRY SPINACH SALAD

This pretty salad is always a hit when I serve it! The recipe came from a cookbook, but I personalized it.
Sometimes just a small change in ingredients can make a big difference.
—*Laura Pounds, Andover, KS*

TAKES: 20 MIN. • **MAKES:** 12 SERVINGS

¼ cup canola oil
¼ cup raspberry vinegar
¼ tsp. Worcestershire sauce
⅓ cup sugar
¼ tsp. paprika
2 green onions, chopped
2 Tbsp. sesame seeds, toasted
1 Tbsp. poppy seeds
12 cups torn fresh spinach
   (about 9 oz.)
2 pints fresh strawberries, halved
4 kiwifruit, peeled and sliced

*Save money by making your own
berry vinegar. Recipe on p. 317.*

1. Place the first 5 ingredients in a blender; cover and process 30 seconds or until blended. Transfer to a small bowl; stir in green onions, sesame seeds and poppy seeds.

2. In a large bowl, combine spinach, strawberries and kiwi. Drizzle with dressing; toss to coat.

1 CUP: 113 cal., 6g fat (1g sat. fat), 0 chol., 76mg sod., 15g carb. (10g sugars, 3g fiber), 2g pro. **DIABETIC EXCHANGES:** 1 vegetable, 1 fat, ½ starch, ½ fruit.

GINGER BEETS & CARROTS

I love fresh garden foods, especially ones as hearty as beets and carrots. This is a delicious way to enjoy a farmers market haul. Plus, the ginger adds both flavor and health benefits.
—*Courtney Stultz, Weir, KS*

TAKES: 25 MIN. • **MAKES:** 4 SERVINGS

Preheat oven to 400°. Place vegetables in a greased 15x10x1-in. baking pan. Whisk remaining ingredients; drizzle over vegetables. Toss to coat. Bake until carrots and beets are crisp-tender, 15-20 minutes.

½ CUP: 92 cal., 5g fat (1g sat. fat), 0 chol., 379mg sod., 12g carb. (8g sugars, 3g fiber), 1g pro. **DIABETIC EXCHANGES:** 1 starch, 1 vegetable.

1½ cups thinly sliced fresh carrots
1½ cups thinly sliced fresh beets
 4 tsp. olive oil
1½ tsp. honey
1½ tsp. ground ginger
 ¾ tsp. soy sauce
 ½ tsp. sea salt
 ½ tsp. chili powder

MY TWO CENTS
"I made it a sheet-pan dinner by adding chicken breasts. I used baby carrots."
—MARYANNET, TASTEOFHOME.COM

CLAM FRITTERS

We had clam fritters every time we went to Rhode Island. This recipe reminds
us of those trips and brings back that memorable taste whenever we want it.
—*Cecelia Wilson, Rockville, CT*

TAKES: 20 MIN. • **MAKES:** 1 DOZEN

⅔ cup all-purpose flour
1   tsp. baking powder
¼   tsp. salt
⅛   tsp. pepper
1   can (6½ oz.) minced clams
1   large egg
3   Tbsp. 2% milk
⅓   cup diced onion
    Oil for deep-fat frying
    Optional: Tartar sauce and
    lemon wedges

*Save money by making your own
tartar sauce. Recipe on p. 312.*

1. In a bowl, combine the flour, baking powder, salt and pepper; set aside. Drain clams, reserving 2 Tbsp. juice; set clams aside. In a small bowl, beat the egg, milk and reserved clam juice; stir into dry ingredients just until moistened. Add the clams and onion.

2. In an electric skillet or deep-fat fryer, heat oil to 375°. Drop batter by tablespoonfuls into oil. Fry for 2-3 minutes or until golden brown, turning occasionally. Drain on paper towels. Serve fritters with tartar sauce and lemon wedges if desired.

1 FRITTER: 73 cal., 4g fat (0 sat. fat), 21mg chol., 176mg sod., 6g carb. (0 sugars, 0 fiber), 3g pro.

ROUND CHEESE BREAD

Who says homemade bread has to be time-consuming to make? Requiring just 10 minutes of prep work, this savory loaf gives you fresh-baked, buttery goodness in a flash.
Deborah Ditz, Medicine Hat, AB

PREP: 10 MIN. • **BAKE:** 20 MIN. + COOLING • **MAKES:** 8 SERVINGS

1½ cups biscuit/baking mix
1 cup shredded part-skim mozzarella cheese
¼ cup grated Parmesan cheese
½ tsp. dried oregano
½ cup 2% milk
1 large egg, room temperature, lightly beaten
2 Tbsp. butter, melted
Additional Parmesan cheese

Save money by making your own biscuit/baking mix. Recipe on p. 304.

1. In a large bowl, combine the biscuit mix, mozzarella cheese, Parmesan cheese, oregano, milk and egg (batter will be thick).

2. Spoon into a greased 9-in. round baking pan. Drizzle with butter; sprinkle with additional Parmesan cheese.

3. Bake at 400° for 20-25 minutes or until a toothpick inserted in the center comes out clean. Cool for 10 minutes. Cut into wedges. Serve warm.

1 PIECE: 183 cal., 10g fat (5g sat. fat), 46mg chol., 440mg sod., 15g carb. (2g sugars, 0 fiber), 7g pro.

TIMESAVING TECHNIQUE

A quick spritz of cooking spray will keep cheese from sticking to the grater. Cleanup is a lot easier.

HONEY & OAT YEAST BREAD

This recipe meets my three most important criteria: It's easy, healthy and kid-approved!
One of my husband's friends shared the directions for this fabulous multigrain bread.
—*Lisa Bedord, Power, MT*

PREP: 30 MIN. + RISING • **BAKE:** 25 MIN. + COOLING • **MAKES:** 1 LOAF (12 PIECES)

½ cup water
6½ tsp. butter, divided
½ cup old-fashioned oats
½ cup unsweetened applesauce
¼ cup honey
1 tsp. salt
2 tsp. active dry yeast
2 Tbsp. warm water (110° to 115°)
1 large egg, room temperature
1½ cups whole wheat flour
1¼ to 1¾ cups all-purpose flour

SAVE SOME CASH

Instead of honey in this recipe, you'll get the same sweetening power by using ⅓ cup granulated sugar. Or use 2 Tbsp. each sugar and molasses to give your bread a kiss of rich taste without the expense of honey.

1. In a small saucepan, bring water and 4½ tsp. butter just to a boil. In a small bowl, pour boiling liquid over oats. Add the applesauce, honey and salt. Let stand until mixture cools to 110°-115°, stirring occasionally.

2. In a large bowl, dissolve yeast in warm water. Add the oatmeal mixture, egg, whole wheat flour and 1 cup all-purpose flour. Beat until smooth. Stir in enough remaining all-purpose flour to form a soft dough (dough will be sticky).

3. Turn onto a floured surface; knead until smooth and elastic, 6-8 minutes. Place in a greased bowl, turning once to grease the top. Cover and let rise in a warm place until doubled, about 1 hour.

4. Punch dough down. Shape into an 8-in. round loaf on a greased baking sheet. Cover and let rise in a warm place until doubled, about 30 minutes.

5. Melt remaining butter; brush over loaf. Bake at 375° for 25-30 minutes or until golden brown. Cool on wire rack.

1 PIECE: 162 cal., 3g fat (2g sat. fat), 23mg chol., 219mg sod., 30g carb. (7g sugars, 3g fiber), 5g pro.

BEET & SWEET POTATO FRIES

Instead of offering traditional french fries, try these oven-baked root vegetables as a flavorful side dish.
—*Marie Rizzio, Interlochen, MI*

PREP: 15 MIN. • **BAKE:** 20 MIN. • **MAKES:** 5 SERVINGS (½ CUP SAUCE)

1. In a small bowl, combine the mayonnaise, peppercorns and ¼ tsp. ground pepper. Cover and refrigerate until serving.

2. Peel and cut sweet potato in half widthwise; cut each half into ½-in. strips. Place in a small bowl. Add 1 Tbsp. oil, ¼ tsp. salt and ⅛ tsp. pepper; toss to coat. Spread onto a parchment-lined baking sheet.

3. Peel and cut beets in half; cut into ½-in. strips. Transfer to the same bowl; add the remaining oil, salt and pepper. Toss to coat. Spread onto another parchment-lined baking sheet.

4. Bake vegetables, uncovered, at 425° for 20-30 minutes or until tender, turning once. Serve with peppercorn mayonnaise.

1 SERVING: 226 cal., 14g fat (2g sat. fat), 8mg chol., 455mg sod., 25g carb (14g sugars, 4g fiber), 3g pro. **DIABETIC EXCHANGES:** 2 starch, 2 fat.

½ cup reduced-fat mayonnaise
1 tsp. pink peppercorns, crushed
½ tsp. green peppercorns, crushed
½ tsp. coarsely ground
     pepper, divided
1 large sweet potato (about 1 lb.)
2 Tbsp. olive oil, divided
½ tsp. sea salt, divided
2 large fresh beets (about 1 lb.)

AU GRATIN PEAS & POTATOES

While this delicious potato skillet is a wonderful side dish, we find it satisfying enough to be a main course too. The skillet preparation takes less time than baking an au gratin casserole or scalloped potatoes—but it's still good old-fashioned comfort food at its best!
—*Marie Peterson, DeForest, WI*

TAKES: 30 MIN. • **MAKES:** 8 SERVINGS

6   bacon strips, diced
1   medium onion, chopped
4   cups peeled cooked
    potatoes, sliced
½   tsp. salt
1   pkg. (10 oz.) frozen peas,
    cooked and drained
2   cups shredded sharp
    cheddar cheese, divided
½   cup mayonnaise
½   cup 2% milk

1. In a large skillet, cook bacon until crisp. Remove with a slotted spoon to paper towels. Drain, reserving 1 Tbsp. drippings. In the drippings, saute onion until tender.

2. Layer with potatoes, salt, peas, 1 cup cheese and bacon. Reduce heat; cover and simmer until heated through, about 10 minutes.

3. Combine mayonnaise and milk until smooth; pour over bacon. Sprinkle with the remaining cheese. Remove from the heat; let stand for 5 minutes before serving.

¾ CUP: 354 cal., 23g fat (8g sat. fat), 43mg chol., 96mg sod., 24g carb. (4g sugars, 3g fiber), 13g pro.

MONKEY MUFFINS

These bite-sized mini muffins will be a favorite with your family and friends—or anyone who loves bananas, peanut butter and chocolate! They are a nice way to use overripe bananas.
—*Amie Longstaff, Painesville Township, OH*

PREP: 20 MIN. • **BAKE:** 15 MIN./BATCH • **MAKES:** 6 DOZEN

1. Preheat oven to 350°. In a large bowl, cream butter and 1 cup sugar until light and fluffy, 5-7 minutes. Add eggs, 1 at a time, beating well after each addition. Beat in the bananas, peanut butter, milk and vanilla. Combine the flour, baking soda and salt; add to creamed mixture just until moistened. Fold in chips.

2. Fill greased or paper-lined miniature muffin cups three-fourths full. Sprinkle with remaining 1 Tbsp. sugar. Bake until a toothpick inserted in the center comes out clean, 14-16 minutes. Cool for 5 minutes before removing from pans to wire racks. Serve warm.

FREEZE OPTION: Wrap muffins in foil and freeze up to 3 months. To use, thaw at room temperature. Warm if desired.

1 MUFFIN: 63 cal., 3g fat (1g sat. fat), 9mg chol., 57mg sod., 8g carb. (5g sugars, 0 fiber), 1g pro.

½   cup butter, softened
1   cup plus 1 Tbsp. sugar, divided
2   large eggs, room temperature
1   cup mashed ripe bananas
⅔   cup peanut butter
1   Tbsp. 2% milk
1   tsp. vanilla extract
2   cups all-purpose flour
1   tsp. baking soda
½   tsp. salt
¾   cup miniature semisweet
    chocolate chips

RAMEN NOODLE SALAD

With added crunch from ramen noodles and sunflower seeds, plus a
sweet, glossy dressing, this lively salad is a definite crowd pleaser!
—*Beverly Sprague, Baltimore, MD*

TAKES: 25 MIN. · **MAKES:** 16 SERVINGS

1. Whisk together first 5 ingredients. Refrigerate, covered, until serving.

2. Discard seasoning packet from noodles or save for another use. Break noodles into small pieces. In a large skillet, heat butter over medium-high heat. Add the noodles; saute until golden brown.

3. Combine romaine, broccoli, onions, sunflower kernels and noodles. Just before serving, whisk dressing and pour over salad; toss to coat.

¾ CUP: 189 cal., 13g fat (3g sat. fat), 4mg chol., 144mg sod., 17g carb. (7g sugars, 2g fiber), 4g pro.

MAKE IT YOUR OWN
Gently fold in a well-drained
can of mandarin oranges
to create a sweet-tart
burst of flavor.

½ cup sugar
½ cup canola oil
¼ cup cider vinegar
1½ tsp. soy sauce
¼ tsp. salt
2 pkg. (3 oz. each) ramen noodles
2 Tbsp. butter
1 bunch romaine, torn (7 cups)
1 bunch broccoli,
   cut into florets (4 cups)
6 green onions, chopped
½ cup sunflower kernels

MY TWO CENTS

"Yummy and so easy to just throw in the slow cooker! Nice flavors."

—LURKY27, TASTEOFHOME.COM

MARMALADE-GLAZED CARROTS

This side dish is ideal when you'd like to serve your vegetables in a different way for a special dinner. Cinnamon and nutmeg season baby carrots that are simmered with orange marmalade and brown sugar.
—Barb Rudyk, Vermilion, AB

PREP: 10 MIN. • **COOK:** 5½ HOURS • **MAKES:** 6 SERVINGS

2 lbs. fresh carrots halved lengthwise and cut into 2-in. pieces
½ cup orange marmalade
3 Tbsp. cold water, divided
2 Tbsp. brown sugar
1 Tbsp. butter, melted
½ tsp. ground cinnamon
¼ tsp. salt
¼ tsp. ground nutmeg
⅛ tsp. pepper
1 Tbsp. cornstarch

1. In a 3-qt. slow cooker, combine the carrots, marmalade, 1 Tbsp. water, brown sugar, butter and seasonings. Cover and cook on low until carrots are tender, 5-6 hours.

2. In a small bowl, combine cornstarch and remaining water until smooth; stir into carrot mixture. Cover and cook on high until thickened, about 30 minutes. Serve with a slotted spoon.

1 SERVING: 159 cal., 2g fat (1g sat. fat), 5mg chol., 252mg sod., 36g carb. (29g sugars, 3g fiber), 1g pro.

BANANA SPLIT FLUFF

This pretty pink mixture, rich with yummy fruit and nuts, is sure to disappear in a hurry.
It's a sweet and speedy treat that can be served as a dessert or salad.
—*Anne Powers, Munford, AL*

TAKES: 10 MIN. • **MAKES:** 10 SERVINGS

In a large bowl, combine the milk and whipped topping until well blended. Fold in pie filling, bananas, pineapple and nuts.

¾ CUP: 374 cal., 13g fat (8g sat. fat), 13mg chol., 62mg sod., 58g carb. (49g sugars, 2g fiber), 5g pro.

1 can (14 oz.) sweetened
   condensed milk
1 carton (12 oz.) frozen
   whipped topping, thawed
1 can (21 oz.) cherry pie filling
3 medium firm bananas,
   cut into chunks
1 can (8 oz.) crushed
   pineapple, drained
½ cup chopped nuts

LENGTHEN BANANAS' RIPENING TIME
Bananas start ripening as soon as they're picked from trees because ethylene gas releases from their stems. But you can wrap the stems with food wrap or aluminum foil to slow down the ripening process. You may see grocery store bunches of bananas with wrapping on the stems.

POTLUCK BAKED BEANS

I acquired this recipe from a dear friend many years ago,
and it has remained a favorite for family get-togethers.
—*Virginia Sander, North Hollywood, CA*

PREP: 10 MIN. • **BAKE:** 30 MIN. • **MAKES:** 12 SERVINGS

4   bacon strips, chopped
1   medium onion, chopped
1   can (28 oz.) baked beans
1   can (16 oz.) kidney beans,
    rinsed and drained
1   can (15 oz.) pinto beans,
    rinsed and drained
½   cup packed brown sugar
⅓   cup ketchup
2   tsp. Worcestershire sauce

1. In a large skillet, saute bacon and onion over medium heat until bacon is crisp; drain. In a large bowl, combine the beans, brown sugar, ketchup, Worcestershire sauce and bacon mixture.

2. Pour into a shallow 2-qt. baking dish coated with cooking spray. Bake at 350° for 30-35 minutes or until heated through.

½ CUP: 192 cal., 2g fat (1g sat. fat), 7mg chol., 528mg sod., 37g carb. (13g sugars, 7g fiber), 8g pro.

CORNBREAD CASSEROLE

Since my husband likes spicy foods, I frequently sprinkle chopped jalapeno peppers over half of this casserole for him.
—*Carrina Cooper, McAlpin, FL*

PREP: 10 MIN. • **BAKE:** 25 MIN. • **MAKES:** 6 SERVINGS

1 can (15¼ oz.) whole kernel corn, drained
1 can (14¾ oz.) cream-style corn
1 pkg. (8½ oz.) cornbread/muffin mix
1 large egg
2 Tbsp. butter, melted
¼ tsp. garlic powder
¼ tsp. paprika

In a large bowl, combine all ingredients. Pour into a greased 11x7-in. baking dish. Bake, uncovered, at 400° for 25-30 minutes or until the top and edges are golden brown.

1 PIECE: 311 cal., 10g fat (4g sat. fat), 54mg chol., 777mg sod., 50g carb. (14g sugars, 3g fiber), 6g pro.

THRIFTY MAIN DISH POSSIBILITIES

Cornbread casserole makes a fantastic side. But you can also make it a main dish by adding protein, veggies and other mix-ins. Jazz up the recipe with whatever leftovers are in your refrigerator, such as chopped cooked bacon, sliced smoked sausage, cubed cooked chicken or ham, and cooked broccoli, peas or cauliflower.

CHAPTER 6
CHEAP SWEETS

Dessert doesn't have to cost a fortune. These budget-friendly treats are sure to bring big smiles to all who taste them.

STRAWBERRY LEMONADE FREEZER PIE

Three simple ingredients mixed together and spread into a graham cracker crust
make magic while your freezer does all the work. Prep this pie ahead and
freeze it overnight or even longer. Feel free to vary the fruit if you'd like!
—*Debbie Glasscock, Conway, AR*

PREP: 15 MIN. + FREEZING • **MAKES:** 8 SERVINGS

1 container (23.2 oz.) frozen
 sweetened sliced strawberries,
 thawed (2½ cups thawed)
1 pkg. (3.4 oz.) instant
 lemon pudding mix
1 carton (8 oz.) frozen
 whipped topping, thawed
1 graham cracker crust (9 in.)
 Optional: Additional whipped
 topping and fresh strawberries

1. In a large bowl, combine strawberries (with juices) and pudding mix; let stand until slightly thickened, about 5 minutes. Fold in whipped topping. Spread into crust.

2. Freeze at least 8 hours or overnight. Let stand 5-10 minutes before serving. If desired, serve with additional whipped topping and fresh strawberries.

1 PIECE: 306 cal., 10g fat (6g sat. fat), 0 chol., 273mg sod., 51g carb. (45g sugars, 2g fiber), 1g pro.

DIY COOKIE CRUST

Instead of buying a ready-made crust, process graham crackers, Oreos, gingersnaps or other cookies to measure 1½ cups fine crumbs. Mix in ¼ cup sugar if desired (may not be needed if using cookies) and ¼ cup melted butter. Press into pie pan and chill 30 minutes to firm up. Or bake at 375° until lightly browned, 8-10 minutes, then cool.

OLD-FASHIONED OATMEAL RAISIN COOKIES

I've been making these cookies for nearly 30 years. The spice cake mix provides a delicious backdrop to the oats and raisins. The treats are an all-time favorite with my family.
—*Nancy Horton, Greenbrier, TN*

PREP: 10 MIN. • **BAKE:** 10 MIN./BATCH • **MAKES:** 7 DOZEN

1. In a large bowl, beat oil and brown sugar until blended. Beat in eggs, then milk. Combine cake mix and oats; gradually add to brown sugar mixture and mix well. Fold in raisins and pecans.

2. Drop by tablespoonfuls 2 in. apart onto greased baking sheets. Bake at 350° until golden brown, 10-12 minutes. Cool for 1 minute before removing to wire racks.

1 COOKIE: 79 cal., 4g fat (1g sat. fat), 7mg chol., 50mg sod., 10g carb. (6g sugars, 1g fiber), 1g pro.

¾   cup canola oil
¼   cup packed brown sugar
2   large eggs
½   cup 2% milk
1   pkg. spice cake mix (regular size)
2   cups old-fashioned oats
2½ cups raisins
1   cup chopped pecans

GREAT PUMPKIN DESSERT

Here's a crowd-pleasing alternative to pumpkin pie that always gets compliments and requests for the recipe. And it's so easy!
—*Linda Guyot, Fountain Valley, CA*

PREP: 10 MIN. • **BAKE:** 1 HOUR • **MAKES:** 16 SERVINGS

1 can (15 oz.) pumpkin
1 can (12 oz.) evaporated milk
3 large eggs, room temperature
1 cup sugar
4 tsp. pumpkin pie spice
1 pkg. yellow cake mix (regular size)
¾ cup butter, melted
1½ cups chopped walnuts
Vanilla ice cream or whipped cream

1. In a large bowl, beat first 5 ingredients until smooth.

2. Transfer to a greased 13x9-in. baking dish. Sprinkle with cake mix and drizzle with butter. Top with walnuts.

3. Bake at 350° for 1 hour or until a knife inserted in the center comes out clean. Serve with ice cream or whipped cream.

1 PIECE: 385 cal., 21g fat (8g sat. fat), 70mg chol., 326mg sod., 44g carb. (30g sugars, 3g fiber), 8g pro.

WASTE NOT

Nuts add buttery crunch, rich flavor and healthy fats to our diets, but they can be expensive. To make sure they don't go bad, store your nuts in the freezer. Corral open and partial bags of nuts into an airtight freezer container. Frozen nuts will keep fresh for 2 years—much longer than they'd last at room temperature.

MANGO RICE PUDDING

Mangoes are my son's favorite fruit, so I was ecstatic to incorporate them into a healthy dessert. You can also use ripe bananas instead of mango, almond extract instead of vanilla or regular milk in place of soy.
—*Melissa McCabe, Victor, NY*

PREP: 5 MIN. • **COOK:** 50 MIN. • **MAKES:** 4 SERVINGS

2 cups water
¼ tsp. salt
1 cup uncooked long grain brown rice
1 medium ripe mango
1 cup vanilla soy milk
2 Tbsp. sugar
½ tsp. ground cinnamon
1 tsp. vanilla extract
Chopped peeled mango, optional

1. In a large heavy saucepan, bring water and salt to a boil; stir in rice. Reduce heat; simmer, covered, 35-40 minutes or until water is absorbed and rice is tender.

2. Meanwhile, peel, seed and slice mango. Mash mango with a potato masher or fork.

3. Stir milk, sugar, cinnamon and mashed mango into rice. Cook, uncovered, on low 10-15 minutes longer or until liquid is almost absorbed, stirring occasionally.

4. Remove from heat; stir in vanilla. Serve warm or cold, with chopped mango if desired.

1 CUP: 275 cal., 3g fat (0 sat. fat), 0 chol., 176mg sod., 58g carb. (20g sugars, 3g fiber), 6g pro.

BUTTERSCOTCH-TOFFEE CHEESECAKE BARS

I had been making lemon cheesecake bars for years and wanted a new flavor combo. Using the original bar as a starting point, I decided to try a butterscotch and toffee version. The results were amazing!
—*Pamela Shank, Parkersburg, WV*

PREP: 15 MIN. • **BAKE:** 30 MIN. + CHILLING • **MAKES:** 2 DOZEN

1. Preheat oven to 350°. In a large bowl, combine the cake mix, pudding mix, oil and 1 egg; mix until crumbly. Reserve 1 cup for topping. Press remaining mixture into an ungreased 13x9-in. baking pan. Bake 10 minutes. Cool completely on a wire rack.

2. In a small bowl, beat cream cheese and sugar until smooth. Add remaining egg; beat on low speed just until combined. Fold in ½ cup toffee bits. Spread over crust. Sprinkle with reserved crumb mixture. Bake 15-20 minutes or until filling is set.

3. Sprinkle with butterscotch chips and remaining ½ cup toffee bits. Return to oven; bake 1 minute longer. Cool on a wire rack 1 hour. Refrigerate 2 hours or until cold. Cut into bars.

1 BAR: 257 cal., 13g fat (6g sat. fat), 31mg chol., 297mg sod., 34g carb. (22g sugars, 0 fiber), 2g pro.

- 1 pkg. yellow cake mix (regular size)
- 1 pkg. (3.4 oz.) instant butterscotch pudding mix
- ⅓ cup canola oil
- 2 large eggs, divided use
- 1 pkg. (8 oz.) cream cheese, softened
- ⅓ cup sugar
- 1 cup brickle toffee bits, divided
- ½ cup butterscotch chips

5i
VALENTINE CUTOUTS

Cool, fruity and creamy, these gelatin treats are richer than plain gelatin and cut easily into whatever shape you'd like. They're a fun finger food that works for any holiday or theme.
—*Annette Ellyson, Carolina, WV*

PREP: 45 MIN. + CHILLING • **MAKES:** 2 DOZEN

In a bowl, dissolve gelatin in water; set aside for 30 minutes. In a small bowl, whisk milk and pudding mix until smooth, about 1 minute. Quickly pour into gelatin; whisk until well blended. Pour into a greased 13x9-in. dish. Chill until set. Cut into cubes or use a heart-shaped cookie cutter.

1 PIECE: 72 cal., 0 fat (0 sat. fat), 1mg chol., 63mg sod., 16g carb. (16g sugars, 0 fiber), 2g pro.

2 pkg. (6 oz. each) cherry
    or raspberry gelatin
2½ cups boiling water
1 cup cold 2% milk
1 pkg. (3.4 oz.) instant
    vanilla pudding mix

PEANUT BUTTER CHOCOLATE POKE CAKE

When my family is planning a get-together, I can count on three or four people to ask if I'm bringing this dessert. If you don't have a chocolate cake mix, use a white or yellow one and stir in 3 Tbsp. baking cocoa.
—Fay Moreland, Wichita Falls, TX

PREP: 20 MIN. • **BAKE:** 25 MIN. + CHILLING • **MAKES:** 20 SERVINGS

1   pkg. chocolate cake mix
    (regular size)
2   tsp. vanilla extract, divided
    Dash salt
⅔   cup creamy peanut butter
2   cans (14 oz. each) sweetened
    condensed milk
1   cup confectioners' sugar
    Topping: Chopped peanut butter-
    filled sandwich cookies,
    peanut butter cups or
    a combination of both

1. Preheat oven to 350°. Prepare cake mix according to package directions, adding 1 tsp. vanilla and salt before mixing batter. Transfer to a greased 13x9-in. baking pan. Bake and cool completely as package directs.

2. Whisk peanut butter and milk until blended. Using the end of a wooden spoon handle, poke holes in cake 2 in. apart. Slowly pour 2 cups peanut butter mixture over cake, filling each hole. Refrigerate cake and remaining peanut butter mixture, covered, until cake is cold, 2-3 hours.

3. Combine remaining vanilla and remaining peanut butter mixture; gradually beat in enough confectioners' sugar to reach a spreading consistency. Spread over cake. Add toppings as desired. Refrigerate leftovers.

1 PIECE: 360 cal., 16g fat (4g sat. fat), 41mg chol., 312mg sod., 49g carb. (40g sugars, 1g fiber), 7g pro.

MY TWO CENTS

"Perfect for those who love peanut butter and chocolate! Made it for a teenage girls' sleepover and it didn't last until the morning. A couple of girls asked me to print out the recipe for their moms."
—QSTICK 79, TASTEOFHOME.COM

FRUIT COCKTAIL BARS

My mother passed this recipe on to me. The moist bars have a delightful fruity taste,
perfect for potlucks in winter and spring when fresh fruit is limited and expensive.
—Linda Tackman, Escanaba, MI

PREP: 15 MIN. • **BAKE:** 20 MIN. + COOLING • **MAKES:** 2½ DOZEN

1½ cups sugar
2 large eggs, room temperature
1 can (15 oz.) fruit cocktail, undrained
1 tsp. vanilla extract
2¼ cups all-purpose flour
1½ tsp. baking soda
1 tsp. salt
1⅓ cups sweetened shredded coconut
1 cup chopped walnuts

GLAZE
½ cup sugar
¼ cup butter, cubed
2 Tbsp. 2% milk
¼ tsp. vanilla extract

1. In a large bowl, beat sugar and eggs until blended. Beat in fruit cocktail and vanilla. Combine the flour, baking soda and salt; add to the creamed mixture until well blended.

2. Pour into a greased 15x10x1-in. baking pan. Sprinkle with coconut and walnuts. Bake at 350° for 20-25 minutes or until a toothpick inserted in the center comes out clean. Cool on a rack for 10 minutes.

3. In a small saucepan, bring the sugar, butter and milk to a boil. Remove from the heat; stir in vanilla. Drizzle over cake. Cool. Cut into bars.

1 SERVING: 161 cal., 6g fat (3g sat. fat), 18mg chol., 174mg sod., 26g carb. (17g sugars, 1g fiber), 3g pro.

TRIPLE CHOCOLATE CANDY CANE COOKIES

This dazzling cookie showcases one of my family's favorite flavors:
peppermint. It's always one of the first to disappear from the cookie tray.
—*Priscilla Yee, Concord, CA*

PREP: 40 MIN. • **BAKE:** 10 MIN./BATCH + COOLING • **MAKES:** ABOUT 3 DOZEN

1. Preheat oven to 350°. In a small bowl, cream butter and sugar until light and fluffy, 5-7 minutes. Beat in egg. In another bowl, whisk flour, cocoa, salt and baking soda; gradually beat into creamed mixture.

2. Shape dough into 1-in. balls; place 2 in. apart on ungreased baking sheets. Flatten to 2-in. rounds with the bottom of a glass. Bake until set (do not overbake), 6-8 minutes. Cool on pans 5 minutes. Remove to wire racks to cool completely.

3. In a microwave, melt semisweet chocolate with 1 tsp. oil; stir until smooth. Dip half of each cookie into chocolate mixture. Melt white chocolate with remaining oil; drizzle over cookies. Sprinkle tops with crushed candy canes; let stand until set.

1 COOKIE: 115 cal., 6g fat (3g sat. fat), 15mg chol., 63mg sod., 15g carb. (9g sugars, 1g fiber), 1g pro.

¾ cup butter, softened
1 cup sugar
1 large egg, room temperature
1¾ cups all-purpose flour
½ cup baking cocoa
¼ tsp. salt
¼ tsp. baking soda
3 oz. semisweet chocolate, chopped
2 tsp. canola oil, divided
3 oz. white baking chocolate, chopped
¼ cup crushed candy canes (about 10 miniature)

SLOW-COOKER LAVA CAKE

I love chocolate. Perhaps that's why this decadent slow-cooker cake
has long been a family favorite. The cake can also be served cold.
—*Elizabeth Farrell, Hamilton, MT*

PREP: 15 MIN. • **COOK:** 2 HOURS + STANDING • **MAKES:** 8 SERVINGS

1   cup all-purpose flour
1   cup packed brown sugar, divided
5   Tbsp. baking cocoa, divided
2   tsp. baking powder
¼   tsp. salt
½   cup fat-free milk
2   Tbsp. canola oil
½   tsp. vanilla extract
⅛   tsp. ground cinnamon
1¼ cups hot water

1. In a large bowl, whisk flour, ½ cup brown sugar, 3 Tbsp. cocoa, baking powder and salt. In another bowl, whisk milk, oil and vanilla until blended. Add to flour mixture; stir just until moistened.

2. Spread into a 3-qt. slow cooker coated with cooking spray. In a small bowl, mix cinnamon and the remaining brown sugar and cocoa; stir in hot water. Pour over batter (do not stir).

3. Cook, covered, on high 2-2½ hours or until a toothpick inserted in the cake portion comes out clean. Turn off slow cooker; let stand 15 minutes before serving.

1 SERVING: 207 cal., 4g fat (0 sat. fat), 0 chol., 191mg sod., 41g carb. (28g sugars, 1g fiber), 3g pro.

MEXICAN HOT CHOCOLATE

This delicious, not-too-sweet hot chocolate is richly flavored with cocoa and delicately seasoned with spices. The blend of cinnamon and chocolate flavors is wonderful!
—*Kathy Young, Weatherford, TX*

TAKES: 10 MIN. • **MAKES:** 4 SERVINGS

1. In a small saucepan, mix cocoa and sugar; stir in water. Bring to a boil. Reduce heat; cook 2 minutes, stirring constantly.

2. Add cinnamon and cloves; stir in milk. Simmer 5 minutes (do not boil). Whisk in vanilla. Pour hot chocolate into mugs; top with whipped cream. Use cinnamon sticks for stirrers.

1 CUP: 156 cal., 7g fat (4g sat. fat), 25mg chol., 92mg sod., 18g carb. (15g sugars, 1g fiber), 7g pro.

¼ cup baking cocoa
2 Tbsp. brown sugar
1 cup boiling water
¼ tsp. ground cinnamon
   Dash ground cloves or nutmeg
3 cups whole milk
1 tsp. vanilla extract
   Whipped cream
   Whole cinnamon sticks

FRUITED DUTCH BABY

This traditional oven-baked pancake is a sensational way to showcase
fruit, and it makes an ideal holiday breakfast or brunch. If you prefer, sprinkle it
with powdered sugar or serve it with canned pie filling or other fruit.
—*Shirley Robertson, Versailles, MO*

TAKES: 30 MIN. • **MAKES:** 6 SERVINGS

---

1 Tbsp. butter
¾ cup all-purpose flour
1 Tbsp. sugar
¼ tsp. salt
3 large eggs, room temperature,
  lightly beaten
¾ cup 2% milk
1½ cups sliced fresh strawberries
2 medium firm bananas, sliced
  Whipped cream, optional
¼ cup sweetened
  shredded coconut, toasted

1. Place butter in a 9-in. pie plate. Place in a 400° oven for 5 minutes or until melted. Meanwhile, in a large bowl, combine the flour, sugar and salt. Stir in eggs and milk until smooth. Pour into prepared pie plate. Bake for 15-20 minutes or until golden brown.

2. In a large bowl, combine strawberries and bananas. Using a slotted spoon, place fruit in center of pancake. Top with whipped cream if desired. Sprinkle with coconut. Serve immediately.

1 PIECE: 203 cal., 7g fat (4g sat. fat), 114mg chol., 170mg sod., 30g carb. (12g sugars, 2g fiber), 7g pro. **DIABETIC EXCHANGES:** 1½ starch, 1 fat, ½ fruit.

SIMPLE SWAP

For a classic spin on a Dutch baby that's also quite easy, squeeze a few lemon wedges over the dessert and dust it generously with confectioners' sugar. No sliced fruit, whipped cream or coconut required!

OATMEAL CINNAMON COOKIES

My family loves these big old-fashioned cookies. They're crisp, yet still chewy in the center, and the cinnamon makes them a little different from typical oatmeal cookies.
—*Anna Brydl, Tobias, NE*

PREP: 15 MIN. • **BAKE:** 10 MIN./BATCH • **MAKES:** 4 DOZEN

1 cup butter, softened
1 cup sugar
1 cup packed brown sugar
2 large eggs, room temperature
1 tsp. vanilla extract
2 cups all-purpose flour
1 tsp. baking soda
1 tsp. ground cinnamon
½ tsp. baking powder
½ tsp. salt
3 cups quick-cooking oats

1. Preheat oven to 350°. In a large bowl, cream butter and sugars until light and fluffy, 5-7 minutes. Beat in eggs and vanilla. Combine flour, baking soda, cinnamon, baking powder and salt; gradually add to creamed mixture and mix well. Stir in oats.

2. Shape into 1½-in. balls. Place 2 in. apart on ungreased baking sheets. Bake until golden brown, 10-12 minutes. Cool 1 minute before removing from pan to wire racks.

1 COOKIE: 109 cal., 4g fat (3g sat. fat), 18mg chol., 91mg sod., 16g carb. (9g sugars, 1g fiber), 2g pro.

MAKE IT YOUR OWN

Favorite mix-ins for oatmeal cookies include raisins, dried cranberries, chopped dried apricots or dates, chopped walnuts or pecans, and chocolate chips (milk, semisweet or white chocolate).

CRUSTLESS PINEAPPLE PIE

I took a favorite pie recipe and substituted canned pineapple for the coconut.
The results were delicious. You can also bake this ahead of time.
—Christi Ross, Guthrie, TX

PREP: 10 MIN. • **BAKE:** 40 MIN. • **MAKES:** 8 SERVINGS

2 cups 2% milk
⅔ cup sugar
½ cup biscuit/baking mix
¼ cup butter, melted
2 large eggs, room temperature
1½ tsp. vanilla extract
Yellow food coloring, optional
2 cans (8 oz. each) crushed
pineapple, well drained
Whipped topping, optional

*Save money by making your own
biscuit/baking mix. Recipe on p. 304.*

1. In a blender, combine the milk, sugar, biscuit mix, butter, eggs, vanilla and, if desired, food coloring; cover and process until smooth. Sprinkle the pineapple into a greased deep-dish 9-in. pie plate. Pour batter over pineapple.

2. Bake at 350° for 40-45 minutes or until a knife inserted in the center comes out clean. Garnish with whipped topping if desired.

1 PIECE: 225 cal., 10g fat (6g sat. fat), 77mg chol., 198mg sod., 30g carb. (25g sugars, 0 fiber), 4g pro.

NEW ENGLAND INDIAN PUDDING

This recipe was inspired by traditional New England Indian pudding. My version is made in the slow cooker instead of baking hours in the oven. Use real molasses—if it's too strong, cut the amount down to ⅓ cup.
—*Susan Bickta, Kutztown, PA*

PREP: 15 MIN. • **COOK:** 3½ HOURS • **MAKES:** 8 SERVINGS

1. In a large bowl, whisk cornbread mix, pudding mix and milk until blended. Add eggs, molasses and spices; whisk until combined. Transfer to a greased 4- or 5-qt. slow cooker. Cover and cook on high for 1 hour.

2. Reduce heat to low. Stir pudding, making sure to scrape sides of slow cooker well. Cover and cook until very thick, 2½-3 hours longer, stirring once per hour. Serve warm, with ice cream or whipped cream if desired.

⅔ CUP: 330 cal., 9g fat (4g sat. fat), 83mg chol., 526mg sod., 51g carb. (36g sugars, 2g fiber), 8g pro.

1 pkg. (8½ oz.) cornbread/muffin mix
1 pkg. (3.4 oz.) instant butterscotch pudding mix
4 cups whole milk
3 large eggs, lightly beaten
½ cup molasses
1 tsp. ground cinnamon
¼ tsp. ground cloves
¼ tsp. ground ginger
   Optional: Vanilla ice cream or sweetened whipped cream

TIMESAVING TECHNIQUE

For easy cleanup, spritz the measuring cup with a little cooking spray before measuring sticky ingredients such as honey and molasses.

MAMAW EMILY'S STRAWBERRY CAKE

My husband loved his mamaw's strawberry cake. He thought no one
could duplicate it. I made it, and it's just as scrumptious as he remembers.
—*Jennifer Bruce, Manitou, KY*

PREP: 15 MIN. • **BAKE:** 25 MIN. + COOLING • **MAKES:** 12 SERVINGS

1   pkg. white cake mix (regular size)
1   pkg. (3 oz.) strawberry gelatin
3   Tbsp. sugar
3   Tbsp. all-purpose flour
1   cup water
½   cup canola oil
2   large eggs
1   cup finely chopped strawberries

FROSTING
½   cup butter, softened
½   cup crushed strawberries
4½ to 5 cups confectioners' sugar

1. Preheat oven to 350°. Line the bottoms of 2 greased 8-in. round baking pans with parchment; grease parchment.

2. In a large bowl, combine cake mix, gelatin, sugar and flour. Add water, oil and eggs; beat on low speed 30 seconds. Beat on medium 2 minutes. Fold in chopped strawberries. Transfer to prepared pans.

3. Bake until a toothpick inserted in center comes out clean, 25-30 minutes. Cool in pans 10 minutes before removing to wire racks; remove paper. Cool completely.

4. For frosting, in a small bowl, beat butter until creamy. Beat in crushed strawberries. Gradually beat in enough confectioners' sugar to reach desired consistency. Spread frosting between layers and over top and sides of cake.

1 PIECE: 532 cal., 21g fat (7g sat. fat), 51mg chol., 340mg sod., 85g carb. (69g sugars, 1g fiber), 4g pro.

SWITCH UP THE LOOK

You'll be smitten with the nostalgic charm of this rich pink buttercream frosting. But for a change of pace, ice the cake with whipped cream or whipped topping and serve it with fresh berries. Save your prettiest strawberries for garnishing the cake. Use second-tier berries for the cake's interior and frosting.

BANANA ORANGE BARS

I have been making these treats for many years. I no longer remember where the recipe came from, but one thing is certain—the bars are always a hit at family get-togethers and parties.
—Mary Sturgis, Hingham, MA

PREP: 15 MIN. • **BAKE:** 25 MIN. + COOLING • **MAKES:** 20 SERVINGS

1. In a large bowl, beat the bananas, sugar, oil and eggs until well blended. In a small bowl, combine the flour, cinnamon, baking powder, salt and baking soda; gradually beat into banana mixture until blended.

2. Pour into a greased 15x10x1-in. baking pan. Bake at 350° for 25-30 minutes or until a toothpick inserted in the center comes out clean. Cool completely on a wire rack.

3. For frosting, cream butter and confectioners' sugar in a large bowl until light and fluffy. Beat in orange juice and zest until smooth; spread evenly over cake.

1 PIECE: 374 cal., 15g fat (4g sat. fat), 50mg chol., 212mg sod., 59g carb. (46g sugars, 1g fiber), 3g pro.

- 2 cups mashed ripe bananas (3 to 4 medium)
- 1⅔ cups sugar
- 1 cup canola oil
- 4 large eggs
- 2 cups all-purpose flour
- 2 tsp. ground cinnamon
- 1 tsp. baking powder
- 1 tsp. salt
- ½ tsp. baking soda

ORANGE BUTTER FROSTING
- 5 Tbsp. butter, softened
- 4½ cups confectioners' sugar
- 5 Tbsp. orange juice
- ½ tsp. grated orange zest

OATMEAL BROWNIES

The recipe makes the most of a handy packaged brownie mix, so these treats are fast to fix.
If you don't have mini M&M's, use chocolate chips instead. Our kids love the rich
fudgy squares with scoops of ice cream.
—*Jennifer Trenhaile, Emerson, NE*

PREP: 15 MIN. • **BAKE:** 25 MIN. + COOLING • **MAKES:** 5 DOZEN

1½ cups quick-cooking oats
1 cup M&M's minis
½ cup all-purpose flour
½ cup packed brown sugar
½ cup chopped walnuts
½ tsp. baking soda
½ cup butter, melted
1 pkg. fudge brownie mix
(13x9-in. pan size)

1. In a large bowl, combine the oats, M&M's, flour, sugar, walnuts, baking soda and butter. Set aside 1 cup for topping. Pat the remaining mixture into a greased 15x10x1-in. baking pan.

2. Prepare brownie batter according to package directions. Spread over the crust. Sprinkle with the reserved oat mixture.

3. Bake at 350° for 25-30 minutes or until a toothpick inserted in the center comes out clean. Cool on a wire rack. Cut into bars.

1 BROWNIE: 116 cal., 6g fat (2g sat. fat), 15mg chol., 66mg sod., 14g carb. (8g sugars, 1g fiber), 2g pro.

LIME CHEESECAKE PIE

This light citrus pie combines two of our favorite dessert flavors—lime and cheesecake.
It's the perfect treat on a hot day—and all the more inviting because
you don't have to heat up the kitchen to prepare it.
—*Vivian Eagleson, Lawrenceville, GA*

PREP: 5 MIN. + CHILLING • **MAKES:** 8 SERVINGS

1 pkg. (8 oz.) cream cheese, softened
1 can (14 oz.) sweetened condensed milk
⅓ cup lime juice
1½ tsp. vanilla extract
1 graham cracker crust (9 in.)
1 carton (8 oz.) frozen whipped topping, thawed (3 cups)
Grated lime zest, optional

In a large bowl, beat cream cheese until smooth. Beat in milk, lime juice and vanilla. Pour into crust. Refrigerate for 2 hours. Spread or pipe with whipped topping; refrigerate 1 hour longer. If desired, garnish with lime zest.

1 PIECE: 447 cal., 24g fat (14g sat. fat), 46mg chol., 274mg sod., 50g carb. (45g sugars, 0 fiber), 7g pro.

MY TWO CENTS
"I used mini graham cracker crusts. The recipe made 11 pies. My kids loved them! I will be making this treat again."
—SCNTBAILEY, TASTEOFHOME.COM

NO-BAKE FUDGY OAT COOKIES

I got this recipe from my mother-in-law back in 1949 and my grown daughter asked me to share it with her so she could make them for Christmas.
—*Elizabeth Hunter, Prosperity, SC*

PREP: 15 MIN. + STANDING • **MAKES:** ABOUT 3 DOZEN

2¼ cups quick-cooking oats
1 cup sweetened shredded coconut
½ cup 2% milk
¼ cup butter, cubed
2 cups sugar
½ cup baking cocoa
1 tsp. vanilla extract

1. In a large bowl, combine oats and coconut; set aside. In a large saucepan, combine milk and butter. Stir in sugar and cocoa. Bring to a boil. Add oat mixture; cook for 1 minute, stirring constantly. Remove from the heat; stir in vanilla.

2. Drop by rounded tablespoonfuls 1 in. apart onto waxed paper. Let cookies stand until set.

1 COOKIE: 92 cal., 3g fat (2g sat. fat), 4mg chol., 19mg sod., 17g carb. (13g sugars, 1g fiber), 1g pro.

MY TWO CENTS

"I loved these as a kid. I made them for my in-laws and they invited me back—to make them again."

—CRICKET115, TASTEOFHOME.COM

5i
OKLAHOMA COCONUT POKE CAKE

Coconut is the star of this cake. You get a double dose, once with the
mixture that soaks into the cake and second with the coconut sprinkled on top.
Don't worry though, it's a nice flavor treat—not too much coconut.
—Taste of Home *Test Kitchen*

PREP: 10 MIN. • **BAKE:** 25 MIN. + COOLING • **MAKES:** 20 SERVINGS

1. Preheat oven to 350°. Prepare and bake cake mix according to package directions, using a 13x9-in. baking pan.

2. Meanwhile, in a small bowl, mix cream of coconut and milk. Remove cake from oven; place on a wire rack. Using a wooden skewer, pierce top of cake to within 1 in. of edge; twist skewer gently to make slightly larger holes. Spoon milk mixture evenly over cake, being careful to fill each hole. Cool completely.

3. Spread whipped topping over cake; sprinkle with shredded coconut. Refrigerate until serving.

1 PIECE: 320 cal., 12g fat (10g sat. fat), 7mg chol., 211mg sod., 50g carb. (40g sugars, 0 fiber), 3g pro.

1   pkg. white cake mix (regular size)
1   can (15 oz.) cream of coconut
1   can (14 oz.) sweetened
     condensed milk
1   carton (16 oz.) frozen whipped
     topping, thawed (6½ cups)
1   cup sweetened shredded coconut

APPLE CORNBREAD CRISP

With its hearty ingredients and quick prep time, this warm apple crisp makes a smart dessert for any fall night. It reminds me of the recipe my grandmother would serve after our big family seafood dinners. It's absolutely wonderful topped with ice cream.
—*Julie Peterson, Crofton, MD*

PREP: 10 MIN. • **BAKE:** 30 MIN. • **MAKES:** 6 SERVINGS

4   cups sliced peeled
    tart apples (4-5 medium)
¾   cup packed brown sugar, divided
1   pkg. (8½ oz.) cornbread/
    muffin mix
½   cup quick-cooking oats
1   tsp. ground cinnamon (or to taste)
5   Tbsp. cold butter, cubed

1. Preheat oven to 350°. Stir together apples and ¼ cup brown sugar. In another bowl, combine cornbread mix, oats, cinnamon and remaining brown sugar. Cut in butter until crumbly.

2. Add ½ cup cornbread mixture to apples. Transfer to a greased 8-in. square baking dish. Sprinkle remaining cornbread mixture over top. Bake until filling is bubbly and topping is golden brown, 30-35 minutes. Serve warm.

1 SERVING: 421 cal., 15g fat (7g sat. fat), 26mg chol., 413mg sod., 70g carb. (43g sugars, 5g fiber), 4g pro.

CHOCOLATE CARAMEL BARS

5i

Taking dessert or another treat to a church or school potluck is never a problem for me. I jump at the chance to offer these rich, chocolaty bars.
—*Steve Mirro, Cape Coral, FL*

PREP: 15 MIN. • **BAKE:** 25 MIN. • **MAKES:** 3 DOZEN

1. In a small saucepan over low heat, melt caramels with ¼ cup milk; stir until smooth. Meanwhile, in a large bowl, cream butter until light and fluffy. Beat in dry cake mix and remaining milk.

2. Spread half the dough into a greased 13x9-in. baking pan. Bake at 350° for 6 minutes; sprinkle with chocolate chips.

3. Gently spread caramel mixture over chips. Drop remaining dough by tablespoonfuls over caramel layer. Return to the oven for 15 minutes. Cool and cut into bars.

1 SERVING: 185 cal., 9g fat (5g sat. fat), 12mg chol., 161mg sod., 26g carb. (19g sugars, 1g fiber), 2g pro.

- 1 pkg. (11 oz.) caramels
- 1 can (5 oz.) evaporated milk, divided
- ¾ cup butter, softened
- 1 pkg. German chocolate cake mix (regular size)
- 2 cups semisweet chocolate chips

CINNAMON-RAISIN BREAD PUDDING

This rich bread pudding recipe goes together in minutes. There's plenty of old-fashioned cinnamon flavor. The treat is sure to become a favorite!
—Edna Hoffman, Hebron, IN

PREP: 5 MIN. + STANDING • **BAKE:** 35 MIN. • **MAKES:** 2 SERVINGS

1. Preheat oven to 350°. Place bread cubes in a greased 2-cup baking dish. In a small bowl, whisk the egg, milk, brown sugar, butter, cinnamon, nutmeg and salt until blended. Stir in raisins. Pour over bread; let stand for 15 minutes or until bread is softened.

2. Bake until a knife inserted in the center comes out clean, 35-40 minutes. Serve the dessert warm.

1 SERVING: 337 cal., 11g fat (6g sat. fat), 133mg chol., 260mg sod., 54g carb. (42g sugars, 3g fiber), 9g pro.

1 cup cubed cinnamon-raisin bread
1 large egg
⅔ cup 2% milk
3 Tbsp. brown sugar
1 Tbsp. butter, melted
½ tsp. ground cinnamon
¼ tsp. ground nutmeg
   Dash salt
⅓ cup raisins

FAVORITE BANANA CREAM PIE

Homemade banana cream pie is my mom's specialty, and this dreamy dessert
has a wonderful banana flavor. It looks so pretty, and it cuts easily too.
—Jodi Grable, Springfield, MO

PREP: 20 MIN. + CHILLING • **COOK:** 25 MIN. + COOLING • **MAKES:** 8 SERVINGS

Dough for single-crust pie
1 cup sugar
¼ cup cornstarch
½ tsp. salt
3 cups 2% milk
2 large eggs, lightly beaten
3 Tbsp. butter
1½ tsp. vanilla extract
2 large firm bananas
1 cup heavy whipping cream, whipped

1. On a lightly floured surface, roll dough to a ⅛-in.-thick circle; transfer to a 9-in. pie plate. Trim crust to ½ in. beyond rim of plate; flute edge. Refrigerate 30 minutes. Preheat oven to 425°.

2. Line crust with a double thickness of foil. Fill with pie weights, dried beans or uncooked rice. Bake on a lower oven rack until edge is golden brown, 20-25 minutes. Remove foil and weights; bake until bottom is golden brown, 3-6 minutes longer. Cool on a wire rack.

3. In a large saucepan, combine sugar, cornstarch, salt and milk until smooth. Cook and stir over medium-high heat until thickened and bubbly. Reduce the heat; cook and stir 2 minutes longer. Remove from heat. Stir a small amount of hot filling into eggs; return all to pan. Bring to a gentle boil; cook and stir for 2 minutes longer.

4. Remove from heat. Gently stir in butter and vanilla. Press plastic wrap onto surface of custard; refrigerate, covered, 30 minutes.

5. Spread half the custard into crust. Slice bananas; arrange over filling. Pour remaining custard over bananas. Spread with whipped cream. Refrigerate 6 hours or overnight.

DOUGH FOR SINGLE CRUST PIE: Combine 1¼ cups all-purpose flour and ¼ tsp. salt; cut in ½ cup cold butter until crumbly. Gradually add 3-5 Tbsp. ice water, tossing with a fork until dough holds together when pressed. Shape into a disk; wrap and refrigerate 1 hour.

1 PIECE: 521 cal., 30g fat (18g sat. fat), 129mg chol., 406mg sod., 57g carb. (35g sugars, 1g fiber), 8g pro.

CHOCOLATE BANANA CREAM PIE: Divide prepared vanilla custard in half. Pour half the custard into crust. Gently stir 4 oz. melted semisweet chocolate into remaining custard. Cover and refrigerate both for 30 minutes. Arrange bananas over vanilla custard; gently spoon chocolate custard over top. Proceed as directed.

CHAPTER 7

HOMEMADE PANTRY STAPLES

If you can't make it to the store, try your hand at making these staples at home. From chicken broth and marinara to baking mix and condiments, your pantry will be stocked in a jiff.

5i
BISCUIT BAKING MIX

You need just four common pantry staples to put together this versatile mix.
I use it in recipes that call for a store-bought baking mix.
—*Tami Christman, Soda Springs, ID*

TAKES: 5 MIN. • **MAKES:** 12 CUPS

In a large bowl, mix the flour, baking powder and salt; cut in shortening until mixture resembles coarse crumbs. Store in an airtight container in a cool, dry place or in the freezer for up to 8 months.

¼ CUP MIX: 159 cal., 8g fat (2g sat. fat), 0 chol., 248mg sod., 18g carb. (0 sugars, 1g fiber), 2g pro.

9 cups all-purpose flour
¼ cup baking powder
1 Tbsp. salt
2 cups shortening

MY TWO CENTS
"What a treasure. Love how my recipes turn out using this biscuit mix."
—JELLYBUG, TASTEOFHOME.COM

HOMEMADE CHICKEN BROTH

For standout gravies and sauces, make your own chicken broth. Turn everything over to the slow cooker for a long simmer and free up the busy stovetop. Use this in any recipes that call for chicken broth or stock.
—Beth Jacobson, Milwaukee, WI

PREP: 15 MIN. • **COOK:** 6 HOURS • **MAKES:** 5 CUPS

1   leftover chicken carcass
1   medium onion, quartered
1   celery rib, coarsely chopped
1   medium carrot, coarsely chopped
2   fresh parsley sprigs or
   ½ tsp. dried parsley
¼ tsp. dried thyme
1   bay leaf
2   garlic cloves, halved
1   tsp. whole peppercorns
6   cups water

1. Place the first 9 ingredients in a 5-qt. slow cooker; add water. Cook, covered, on low 6-8 hours to allow flavors to blend.

2. Strain broth through a cheesecloth-lined colander; discard vegetables, bones, herbs and peppercorns. If using immediately, skim fat. Or, cool the broth, then refrigerate 8 hours or overnight; remove fat from surface before using. (Broth may be refrigerated up to 3 days or frozen 4-6 months.)

1 CUP: 25 cal., 0 fat (0 sat. fat), 0 chol., 130mg sod., 2g carb. (0 sugars, 0 fiber), 4g pro.

RED LENTIL SOUP MIX

Give your friends the gift of good health. Red lentils are protein powerhouses and are loaded with folate, iron and fiber. Oh, and this soup tastes amazing too.
—Taste of Home *Test Kitchen*

PREP: 25 MIN. • **COOK:** 25 MIN. • **MAKES:** 4 BATCHES (4 CUPS PER BATCH)

¼ cup dried minced onion
2 Tbsp. dried parsley flakes
2 tsp. ground allspice
2 tsp. ground cumin
2 tsp. ground turmeric
1½ tsp. salt
1 tsp. garlic powder
1 tsp. ground cardamom
1 tsp. ground cinnamon
1 tsp. pepper
½ tsp. ground cloves
2 pkg. (1 lb. each) dried red lentils

ADDITIONAL INGREDIENTS (FOR EACH BATCH)
1 medium carrot, finely chopped
1 celery rib, finely chopped
1 Tbsp. olive oil
2 cans (14½ oz. each) vegetable broth

Combine the first 11 ingredients. Place 1⅓ cups lentils in each of four 12-oz. jelly jars. Evenly divide onion mixture among small cellophane bags; place sealed bags inside jars, on top of lentils. Store in a cool, dry place up to 6 months.

TO PREPARE ONE BATCH: Rinse lentils and drain. In a large saucepan over medium-high heat, saute carrot and celery in oil until tender. Add the lentils, onion mixture and broth. Bring to a boil. Reduce heat; simmer, covered, until lentils are tender, 10-15 minutes.

1 CUP: 257 cal., 4g fat (1g sat. fat), 0 chol., 1067mg sod., 42g carb. (4g sugars, 7g fiber), 14g pro.

MY TWO CENTS
"Just delicious. A bit different from other soups I've tried, but we really enjoyed it. Leftovers are terrific the next day too."
—HISTORYGIRL, TASTEOFHOME.COM

5i
40-MINUTE HAMBURGER BUNS

Here on our ranch, I cook for three men who love burgers. These fluffy hamburger buns are just right for their big appetites. The buns are so good that I also serve them plain with a meal.
—*Jessie McKenney, Twodot, MT*

PREP: 20 MIN. + RESTING • **BAKE:** 10 MIN. • **MAKES:** 1 DOZEN

1. In a large bowl, dissolve yeast in warm water. Add oil and sugar; let stand for 5 minutes. Add the egg, salt and enough flour to form a soft dough.

2. Turn onto a floured surface; knead until smooth and elastic, 3-5 minutes. Do not let rise. Divide into 12 pieces; shape each into a ball. Place 3 in. apart on greased baking sheets. Preheat oven to 425°.

3. Cover and let rest for 10 minutes. Bake until golden brown, 8-12 minutes. Remove from pans to wire racks to cool.

1 BUN: 195 cal., 7g fat (1g sat. fat), 18mg chol., 204mg sod., 29g carb. (5g sugars, 1g fiber), 5g pro.

2 Tbsp. active dry yeast
1 cup plus 2 Tbsp. warm water (110° to 115°)
⅓ cup canola oil
¼ cup sugar
1 large egg, room temperature
1 tsp. salt
3 to 3½ cups all-purpose flour

MAKE IT YOUR OWN

These hamburger buns are ultra customizable. In the *Taste of Home* Test Kitchen, we like to add sesame or poppy seeds. To add seeds, brush warm buns with butter and add your favorite toppings. This recipe can also be used to make slider buns or rolls. To make rolls, divide dough into 24 portions, then bake rolls until golden brown.

PESTO

Homemade pesto always makes a thoughtful hostess gift. Mix things up with the cilantro variation.
—Taste of Home *Test Kitchen*

TAKES: 10 MIN. • **MAKES:** ¾ CUP

In a food processor, puree all ingredients. Refrigerate for several weeks or freeze in a tightly covered container. Toss a couple tablespoons pesto with hot cooked pasta.

2 TBSP.: 97 cal., 10g fat (2g sat. fat), 3mg chol., 114mg sod., 1g carb. (0 sugars, 0 fiber), 2g pro.

1 cup tightly packed
  fresh basil or cilantro leaves
1 cup tightly packed
  fresh parsley leaves
1 to 2 garlic cloves
½ cup olive oil
½ cup grated Parmesan cheese
¼ tsp. salt

⑤ⅰ
LEMON-GARLIC HUMMUS

Whipping up this smooth and creamy bean dip requires just five ingredients.
It's a delicious part of our family's Christmas Eve party every year.
—Kris Capener, Ogden, UT

TAKES: 10 MIN. • **MAKES:** 1½ CUPS

¾ cup olive oil
2 cups canned garbanzo beans or
   chickpeas, rinsed and drained
3 Tbsp. lemon juice
2 tsp. minced garlic
½ tsp. salt
   Pita bread wedges or
   assorted fresh vegetables

In a blender or food processor, combine the oil, beans, lemon juice, garlic and salt; cover and process until smooth. Transfer to a small bowl. Serve with pita wedges or vegetables.

¼ CUP: 324 cal., 29g fat (3g sat. fat), 0 chol., 309mg sod., 14g carb. (2g sugars, 3g fiber), 3g pro.

TIMESAVING TECHNIQUE

It's faster to puree the hummus in a blender than in a food processor. A blender will also make a smoother hummus.

CLASSIC TARTAR SAUCE

You'll never buy the jarred stuff again once you've tried this homemade tartar sauce recipe!
—*Michelle Stromko, Darlington, MD*

TAKES: 10 MIN. • **MAKES:** 1 CUP

In a small bowl, combine all ingredients. Cover and refrigerate until serving.

2 TBSP.: 93 cal., 10g fat (2g sat. fat), 1mg chol., 167mg sod., 1g carb. (0 sugars, 0 fiber), 0 pro.

⅔ cup chopped dill pickles
½ cup mayonnaise
3 Tbsp. finely chopped onion
Dash pepper

MONEY-SAVING TIP

Save money and fridge space by making your own mayonnaise-based condiments. Use the following mayo mix-ins to create these gourmet sauces:

• **Aioli:** minced or roasted garlic, lemon juice

• **Dijonnaise:** Dijon mustard, lemon juice, salt, pepper

• **Honey-Mustard Sauce:** honey, yellow or Dijon mustard, lemon juice

• **Remoulade:** spicy mustard, chopped pickles, pickle juice, hot sauce, garlic, paprika

• **Sriracha Mayo:** Sriracha chili sauce, lemon juice, garlic, salt

MARINARA SAUCE

This quick and easy homemade marinara sauce is my kids' favorite.
It works fantastic with spaghetti, and my kids love it in meatball subs too.
—*Cara Bjornlie, Detroit Lakes, MN*

TAKES: 30 MIN. • **MAKES:** 7 CUPS

In a large saucepan, heat oil over medium heat. Add onion; cook and stir until softened, 3-4 minutes. Add garlic; cook 1 minute longer. Add tomatoes, Italian seasoning, sugar, salt and pepper; bring to a boil. Reduce heat; simmer, covered, 10 minutes.

ABOUT ¾ CUP: 91 cal., 2g fat (0 sat. fat), 0 chol., 489mg sod., 12g carb. (8g sugars, 3g fiber), 3g pro. **DIABETIC EXCHANGES:** 2 vegetable, ½ fat.

- 1 Tbsp. olive oil
- 1 small onion, chopped
- 2 garlic cloves, minced
- 2 cans (28 oz. each) Italian crushed tomatoes
- 1 Tbsp. Italian seasoning
- 1 to 2 Tbsp. sugar
- ½ tsp. salt
- ½ tsp. pepper

HOMEMADE TORTILLAS

*I usually have to double this recipe because we go through these so quickly.
The tortillas are so tender, chewy and simple, you'll never use store-bought again.*
—*Kristin Van Dyken, Kennewick, WA*

TAKES: 30 MIN. • **MAKES:** 8 TORTILLAS

2 cups all-purpose flour
½ tsp. salt
¾ cup water
3 Tbsp. olive oil

1. In a large bowl, combine flour and salt. Stir in water and oil. Turn onto a floured surface; knead 10-12 times, adding a little flour or water if needed to achieve a smooth dough. Let rest for 10 minutes.

2. Divide dough into 8 portions. On a lightly floured surface, roll each portion into a 7-in. circle.

3. In a greased cast-iron or other heavy skillet, cook tortillas over medium heat until lightly browned, about 1 minute on each side. Serve warm.

1 TORTILLA: 159 cal., 5g fat (1g sat. fat), 0 chol., 148mg sod., 24g carb. (1g sugars, 1g fiber), 3g pro. **DIABETIC EXCHANGES:** 1½ starch, 1 fat.

SMART SWAP

You can boost the tortillas' fiber content by about 5 times by swapping 1 cup whole wheat flour for 1 cup all-purpose flour. Store whole wheat flour in the refrigerator in a resealable bag or container (to keep out odors). Cold temperatures keep the flour fresh for longer.

THIN CRUST PIZZA DOUGH

My family loves pizza, and this crust is our go-to recipe.
It is healthier and less expensive than delivery and tastes so much better.
—*Theresa Rohde, Scottville, MI*

PREP: 10 MIN. + RESTING • **MAKES:** 2 LBS. (ENOUGH FOR FOUR 12-IN. PIZZAS)

3½ cups bread flour
1 cup whole wheat flour
5 tsp. quick-rise yeast
1 tsp. salt
1 tsp. honey
1½ to 1⅔ cups warm water
(120° to 130°)

THRIFTY TIP

While this recipe makes four 12-in. thin pizza crusts, you can also split the dough in half to make 2 pizzas with thick (deep-dish) crusts.

1. Place flours, yeast and salt in a food processor; pulse until blended. Add honey. While processing, gradually add water until a ball forms. Continue processing 60 seconds to knead dough.

2. Turn dough onto a floured surface; shape into a ball. Cover; let rest 10 minutes. Divide dough into quarters. Use immediately or freeze for later use.

FREEZE OPTION: Place each portion of dough in an airtight container; freeze up to 1 month. To use, thaw in the refrigerator overnight. Proceed as directed.

⅛ OF 1 PIZZA CRUST: 59 cal., 0 fat (0 sat. fat), 0 chol., 89mg sod., 13g carb. (0 sugars, 1g fiber), 3g pro.

TO MAKE PIZZA: Preheat oven to 450°. Grease a 12-in. pizza pan; sprinkle with cornmeal. On a lightly floured surface, stretch and shape 1 portion of dough to form a 12-in. crust; transfer to prepared pan. Top as desired. Bake 15-20 minutes or until crust is lightly browned. If using frozen dough, thaw in the refrigerator overnight. Proceed as directed.

5i
BERRY VINEGAR

For a delicious vinegar for salad dressings and marinades, try this vinegar with cranberries.
It would make a wonderful dressing base for a side salad during the holidays.
—*Losloy Colgan, London, ON*

TAKES: 25 MIN. • **MAKES:** 1½ CUPS

In a saucepan, bring all ingredients to a boil. Reduce heat and simmer for 5 minutes or until the cranberries burst. Cool. Strain through a fine sieve into sterilized bottles or jars. Seal tightly. Discard cranberries and cinnamon stick. Chill until ready to use in your vinegar-and-oil salad dressing.

2 TBSP.: 62 cal., 0 fat (0 sat. fat), 0 chol., 0 sod., 16g carb. (15g sugars, 1g fiber), 0 pro.

BERRY VINAIGRETTE: Mix ¼ cup Berry Vinegar, ¾ cup olive oil, ½ tsp. Dijon mustard and ⅛ tsp. pepper. Season with salt or sugar if desired.

¾   cup white vinegar
¾   cup water
¾   cup sugar
1   cinnamon stick
1   pkg. (12 oz.) fresh or
     frozen cranberries

RECIPE INDEX